The Urban Forager

CULINARY EXPLORING & COOKING ON L.A.'S EASTSIDE

Elisa Callow

PHOTOGRAPHY BY
ANN ELLIOTT CUTTING

Advance Praise

"Elisa Callow takes us on a stroll through her kitchen, her neighborhood, and her meandering path of learning to be a great cook—and drops a lot of knowledge along the way. I relished her discoveries and expanded my own world of food and community."

ANNA THOMAS, JAMES BEARD AWARD WINNER AND AUTHOR OF *THE VEGETARIAN EPICURE*, *LOVE SOUP*, AND *VEGAN VEGETARIAN OMNIVORE*

"If indeed the kitchen is the heart of the home, *The Urban Forager* wonderfully captures this truth with warm, anecdotal stories, delicious food photographs, and charming illustrations. As a chef, I read and use lots of recipes on a daily basis, and Elisa's recipes are manageable, smart, and well tested. The creatively selected ingredients coupled with didactic methods teach the user how to develop into a skilled cook. *The Urban Forager* is much more than a collection of fabulous recipes—it is a lifestyle book."

ONIL CHIBÁS, CHEF/OWNER, ONIL CHIBÁS EVENTS

"Elisa has always known the way to the hidden jewels in our culture-rich city. This stunning treasure map focuses on her friends, family, and a beautiful life as she takes us through her community, to the people and places that inspire her love of food. The book is also bursting with warm, lovingly composed photos and recipes. How lucky we all are to go with her on this journey."

CHRISTINE MOORE, AUTHOR OF *LITTLE FLOWER BAKING* AND *LITTLE FLOWER: RECIPES FROM THE CAFÉ*

"I'm untrained in the kitchen but I still like to cook. When I skeptically picked up *The Urban Forager*, I was pleasantly surprised to find that Elisa Callow had me covered on all my weakest fronts, from what to keep on hand to how to plan so I can actually cook as effectively as I pick up takeout. Most importantly for this Angeleno, *The Urban Forager* is firmly rooted in L.A.'s multicultural stew—more specifically, its Eastside mélange. This is not just a cookbook, it's a guidebook that takes you into new markets, opens doors to new taste sensations, and introduces you to wonderful chefs representing a wide variety of cultural influences. I can't wait to eat my way through *The Urban Forager*—to explore the food, the cultures, the people, and the wonderful sense of sharing that Elisa brings to these pages." AARON PALEY, PRESIDENT OF COMMUNITY ARTS RESOURCES (CARS) IN LOS ANGELES, FOUNDING EXECUTIVE DIRECTOR OF CICLAVIA, AND FOUNDER OF THE L.A. NONPROFIT YIDDISHKAYT

"I only wish that I had been gifted this book sooner! The beautiful photos and simple, easy-to-follow recipes inspire me to cook and eat. My favorite parts are the concentric circles of culinary influence, encouraging each of us to explore our own neighborhoods and beyond, support small businesses, and, most importantly, explore communities outside of our own. Food and the culinary arts are the best way to get to know other people and form closer bonds, whether it be with family, a neighbor, a community member, or even a stranger. This book embodies this full spirit." LESLIE ITO, EXECUTIVE DIRECTOR, ARMORY CENTER FOR THE ARTS, AND LIFELONG FOOD AND CULTURE ADVOCATE

"Elisa Callow offers a gorgeously inspiring collection of recipes that provides both basics for the novice and innovations for the experienced. Equal parts rustic and elegant, this book is stuffed with many delectable recipes designed to satisfy hunger pangs from simple to sophisticated. Gorge yourself on the beautiful photos and loving illustrations; devour the odes to eastside tastemakers. Then choose a dish that sings to you, roll up your sleeves, and dive in!" DÉSIRÉE ZAMORANO, AUTHOR OF *THE AMADO WOMEN* AND *THE RESTLESS CHEF* BLOG

Published by
Prospect Park Books
2359 Lincoln Avenue
Altadena, California 91001
www.prospectparkbooks.com

PROSPECT
·PARK·
BOOKS

Distributed by Consortium Books Sales & Distribution www.cbsd.com

Library of Congress Cataloging in Publication Data is on file with the Library of Congress
The following is for reference only:
Callow, Elisa
The Urban Forager: Culinary Exploring & Cooking on L.A.'s Eastside / by Elisa Callow — 1st ed.
p. cm.
ISBN: 978-1-945551-42-0
1. Cooking. 2. Cooking, California. 3. Cooking, Los Angeles, CA. I. Title.

CREDITS:
EDITOR: Colleen Dunn Bates
COPY EDITOR: Anna Ganahl
DESIGN: Marika van Adelsberg
PHOTOGRAPHS: Ann Elliott Cutting
PORTRAIT OF ELISA CALLOW AND ANN ELLIOTT CUTTING: Dennis Keeley
ILLUSTRATIONS:
    Grandson Anthony James Durham, *line drawings pages* 26, 68, 80, 106, 118, 142, 170, 198
    Severin Grant, *line drawings pages* 17, 27, 135
    Simone Rein, *color illustrations pages* 24, 25, 104, 105, 140, 141, 168, 169, 196, 197, 228
SERVING DISHES: Ann Elliott Cutting—cover, 29, 41, 47, 50, 55, 73, 74, 79, 120, 126, 131, 146, 172,
    175, 186

First edition, first printing
Printed in China by Imago on sustainably produced, FSC-certified paper

Table of Contents

Sunday morning at the Porch Market in Altadena. Steve Hofvendahl and Lily Knight host an occasional market of beautiful fruits, baked goods, live music, and fellowship. The schedule changes, based on their time and the orchard's yield. Email Steve at hodaddyo@sbcglobal.net for market-day notification.

Thanks to the Inspiring Cooks in My Life Who Have Contributed to This Cookbook

Jack Aghoian, eastside food maker, cofounder of Jack's Kasbah; neighbor

Julia Breithaupt, longtime friend from Germany; food lover

Charlotte Callow, Eric's mother

David Callow, Eric's brother

Eric Callow, my husband

Sumi Chang, eastside food maker; founder of Europane Bakery

Arpy Gendahl, friend

Margie Greben, my stepmom

Barbara Lefton Herman, dearest friend; we met in middle school

Doug Herman, friend; Barbara's husband

Alyse Jacobson, jam-making expert; started me on my 200-jar-a-year obsession

Lily Knight, friend; coproducer of the Porch Market

Sylvia Lefton, friend; Barbara Herman's mother

Rumi Mahmood, eastside food maker; co-omnivore gourmet

Francesca Mallus, chef and teacher

Tomasa Mendoza, friend

Shirley Moore, friend of Margie and Seymour Greben, my stepmom and dad

Bernice "Beanie" Palmer, Eric's aunt; Charlotte Callow's sister

Minh Phan, eastside food maker; founder of Field Trip and porridge + puffs

Mario Rodriguez, eastside food maker; co-enjoyer of all things delicious

Sylvia Poitrier Sobbotke, friend in Germany; her Alsatian roots are evident in her cooking

Peggy Spear, friend

Taka Suzuki, friend

RECIPE TESTERS:

Bill Anawalt, friend

Christiana Thomas, friend; former baker

John Callow, Eric's son; my stepson

Juno Chimera, friend

Masako Yatabe Thomsen, baking partner of Sumi Chang; supreme Japanese cook

Betsy Clancy, Anna Ganahl's sister

Noriko Gamblin, friend

Désirée Zamorano, friend; fearless cooking partner

Anna Ganahl, friend

Elisa Hamed, cousin

Doris Hausmann, friend

Esther Kang, friend

Kaitlin Corunelle Krusoe, friend

Richard Ramos, David Spiro's husband

Liana Soifer, friend

David Spiro, friend

With Gratitude to My Community

A DEFINITION:

ur·ban *adj.*
In, relating to, or characteristic of
a city or town. "The urban
population."
Synonyms: town, city, municipal, civic,
metropolitan, built-up, downtown.

for·age *v.*
1. The act of looking or searching for food
   or provisions.
2. To wander in search of food or
   provisions.
3. To conduct a search; rummage.
4. Informal: To obtain by foraging:
   "foraged a snack from the refrigerator."

urban forager
1. Searchers for provisions in towns and
   cities.
2. Those who uncover the rare and
   wonderful.

I created this book with novice and adventurous cooks in mind, in the hope that it teaches, inspires, and leads to a new trove of food memories. There is no better place than L.A.'s eastside to begin a cooking journey. In my mind, its food culture is one of the most interesting and exciting anywhere—a culture jump-started and sustained by a growing corps of fearless chefs whose techniques, ingredients, and tastes are challenged and refreshed by our increasingly diverse community.

While many cookbooks drop the reader into the middle of intensely complex and arcane recipes, I designed this one as a bridge to the unfamiliar—beginning with basic techniques and building-block recipes, some of which reappear in subsequent chapters as key ingredients. *The Urban Forager* sets forth recipes from my own kitchen along with beloved recipes from great cooks, friends, and family; provides a carefully curated list of our region's one-of-a-kind neighborhood food shops offering quality ingredients and inviting culinary exploration; and suggests ways to expand your own cooking repertoire.

With the exception of baking and its exacting requirements, I see recipes as open-ended guides. The more you cook, the more secure you become in trying something new. Variations come from both imagination and desperation—and may also be inspired by an emerging commitment to use food wisely and without waste. I call similar ingredients from familiar or different cooking cultures "flavor cousins," and identify ways that an item in your refrigerator or pantry or an experience with a new taste or cuisine can find its way into your cooking. Think the sweet Chinese sausage so much like pepperoni (but even more delicious), beet greens that can be exchanged for kale or chrysanthemum greens, a fat slice of Oaxacan egg-infused bread spread with butter and sugar that is equivalent to a brioche, a tiny dollop of tamarind paste that could double as dried apricots or plums and adds umami to a chicken marinade or baked winter squash. Watch for the *Try This* key to recipe variations throughout the cookbook.

As a centerpiece, I profile five of the eastside's most inspiring and creative food makers: Sumi Chang, master baker and founder of Pasadena's Europane; Minh Phan, inventive creator of porridge + puffs in Filipinotown; and brilliant home cooks Mario Rodriguez, Rumi Mahmood, and Jack Aghoian. I hope that the sampling of their recipes, ingredient resources, and food journeys throughout this book will inspire your cooking repertoire as they have mine.

Cooking has led me to connect with new neighborhoods and cultures, and it is this sense-filled passage that has continually energized me on my journey to become a confident and proficient cook. L.A.'s eastside is truly an area rich in deeply-rooted cultures, and its food echoes this variety, yielding an amazing number of choices, from an emerging small-farms community in Altadena to several high-quality Armenian, Mexican, and Asian markets. There are elegant cheese stores, excellent bakeries, and a fair share of farmers' markets. Most are one-of-a-kind businesses where the owner's pride is evident in the quality of the merchandise.

I also understand that to be a true urban forager, deep curiosity must override fear and self-consciousness; the desire for learning takes precedence. I find myself in the optimum state of the beginner's mind as I push myself into markets where ninety percent of what I see is a mystery. In many foraging expeditions, my puzzled face becomes an invitation for acts of kindness and welcome in the stores I enter. Without fail, I am approached by a variation on the *nonna*/grandma/*bà nội*, whose knowledge of a particular cuisine is as deep as her desire to teach. Whether you live in a big city or small town, your explorations will undoubtedly yield similarly satisfying discoveries, culinary treasures, and connection.

I hope that each one of you will find your delight by exploring this collection of ideas, recipes, and resources that originated from my personal history—one that continues to deepen and evolve through my city's growing community of generous and inspiring food makers.

Nothing feels better than making a delicious meal, slowly and with care, and then sharing it with others.

Getting Started: An Appeal for Planning

Over the past few years, I have found ready-made food to be less and less satisfying compared with homemade dishes. While homemade can mean more work, the benefits far outweigh the time required. Let's consider two scenarios.

SCENARIO ONE: THE READY-MADE DINNER

What you do: Purchase roasted chicken, boxed pilaf, frozen peas, salad in a bag, and bottled ranch dressing after work for dinner that evening. (Note: For a family of four there will be no leftovers, as most precooked chickens are on the small size. They are rarely organic.)

Total time: 45 to 60 minutes (includes driving to the store, selecting food, waiting in line, driving home, cooking the peas and pilaf).

CALORIE COUNT: 600 to 1,200, depending on number of servings.

SCENARIO TWO: DINNER MADE BY YOU

What you do: The day before your evening meal, you purchase one organic roasting chicken, butternut squash, a fresh lemon, and two heads of organic red leaf lettuce. You have on hand olive oil and vegetable oil, sherry vinegar, soy sauce, long-grain rice, butter, black pepper, garlic, and canned chicken broth.

That day or evening, you marinate the chicken pieces in a mixture of vegetable oil, soy sauce, crushed garlic, salt, and lemon juice and store in a Pyrex container. You halve the butternut squash, seed each half, brush with olive oil, add salt and store in the refrigerator until ready to cook.

The day of dinner, you roast the chicken and bake the squash at the same time. You make a double recipe of vinaigrette with olive oil, garlic, sherry vinegar, and salt and pepper. And you make a double recipe of pilaf by adding a tablespoon of butter to the saucepan, adding the rice, and cooking until golden, then adding hot chicken broth and simmering on low heat for 15 minutes.

TOTAL TIME: 55 minutes (includes shopping and active cooking time, prep the night before, and final steps the day of the evening meal. It does not count the roasting time, which requires none of your attention except to check for doneness).

CALORIE COUNT: 450 to 900, depending on the number of servings.

As this chicken is larger, you should have enough cooked chicken and rice for a second one-dish meal, such as chicken and rice soup (for four), chicken salad (for four), or chicken enchiladas (for four), thus saving time, energy, and $$$, as well as being assured of the quality of the ingredients.

NOW, COMPARE THE SCENARIOS

There is little difference in time expended; rather it has more to do with planning. Imagine how much better you might feel at the end of a workday knowing that most of dinner is waiting for you. All you have to do is roast the chicken and the squash while you relax, change your clothes, help your kids do their homework, take a walk—anything but wait in line at the supermarket at the busiest time of the day. Leftovers are transformed and elevated into a completely new meal on night two. Enough said.

WHAT TO KEEP ON HAND

Once you become more secure with cooking techniques, you will waste less and might even find yourself experimenting more freely with ingredients. I have learned from years of cooking for myself, my family, and friends that certain ingredients are key to many dishes. Having these "food tools" on hand allows me to be creative without a great deal of effort or last-minute running around. The list below is designed to help you develop your own kitchen as a place for inspiration, confidence, and readiness.

ON THE COUNTER
Avocados
Bread, homemade or from a great bakery
Citrus fruits, including lemons and limes
Garlic, ginger, onions, shallots
Potatoes of various types, yams
Stone fruits such as peaches, apricots, plums
Tomatoes

IN THE REFRIGERATOR
Butter
Cheeses: whole parmesan, gruyère, goat, jack, manchego, cotija, feta
Crème fraîche, mayonnaise, and yogurt
Eggs
Fruits and vegetables requiring refrigeration, such as lettuce, fresh herbs, and
   summer squashes
Masa for tortillas
Mustards: Dijon and yellow
Whole milk, buttermilk, and cream (avoid ultra-pasteurized; much of the good bacteria
   that creates cultured-milk products, such as crème fraîche and yogurt, are destroyed)
Wine and bubbly water
Yeast
Why no juices? Because they are full of sugar without the positive nutritional benefits
   of fresh fruit's fiber.

IN THE FREEZER
Chicken, cut up
Chili, homemade, or other dishes that freeze well, such as beans and soups without
   dairy ingredients
Cookie rolls, homemade (ready to bake)
Garam masala and any other spice mixes
Ice cream
Nuts, especially high-oil nuts that can become rancid easily, such as walnuts and
   pecans

Pancetta, an Italian bacon that adds complexity of flavor to many dishes, especially
soups and stews
Rolls, good-quality (for last-minute needs)
Sausages: good-quality pork, turkey, chicken, including chorizo, lap cheong, breakfast
Spices and dried chiles, all types

IN THE PANTRY

I buy most of these items in bulk and store them in large jars, a practice that saves a lot of money and is environmentally more responsible, as it avoids excessive packaging.

Anchovies packed in oil
Beans: garbanzo, black, pinto, kidney (dried and canned)
Bulgur wheat
Capers
Chicken broth, canned or boxed
Chocolate chips and baking chocolate
Coconut milk
Dried fruit: raisins, cranberries, apricots
Extracts: vanilla and almond
Flour: white, pastry, rye, bread
Flour for pasta: oo (finely milled) and semolina (coarsely milled durum wheat)
Lentils of various colors
Nuts, roasted, such as almonds
Oats, whole
Oils: grapeseed, olive, sesame
Pasta, dried, several varieties
Polenta, quinoa
Rice: long-grain, short-grain, black
Salt: iodized, kosher, sea
Soy sauce, fish sauce, hoisin sauce
Spices, ground: mustard and paprika (store up to six months)
Spices, whole: allspice, black pepper, cardamom, caraway seeds, cinnamon, cloves,
cumin, fennel seeds, mustard seeds, nutmeg, saffron
Sugars: granulated, brown, honey, molasses, maple syrup
Tamarind paste
Tomatoes: canned, sun-dried, sauce
Vinegars: sherry, champagne, apple cider, red wine

It is worth paying a bit more for good storage items, including glass and good-quality plastic containers, as well as resealable bags for the refrigerator and freezer. The investment will be made up in food that remains fresh. I don't recommend using glass in the freezer, as liquid expands as it freezes and can cause glass to crack.

HERBS TO GROW

California has a year-round outdoor growing season. In colder climates, plant in a generous-size pot that can be moved indoors or outdoors, depending on the temperature.

Basil (spring and summer)	Parsley (all year)
Tarragon (spring and summer)	Rosemary (all year)
Chives (all year)	Thyme and/or oregano (all year)
Marjoram (all year)	

A WORD ON FOOD SOURCES

Recent news about the origins of food, how it is processed, and its safety should not be taken lightly. Paying less for poor ingredients is a false economy, as you can end up with food that does not taste good or store well because it is not fresh.

Chicken and beef are often raised in cruel environments, and ranching has proved to be one of the most environmentally degrading processes affecting our water and land. In some cases, particularly with meat and eggs, you are eating food that has been raised with growth-producing hormones that may be linked to breast and other cancers.

Imagine what it requires to raise a cow versus a row of lettuce!

So consider eating more grains, fruits, and vegetables, and include meat as a condiment rather than the centerpiece of your meal. You will save money, possibly lose weight, and, if you eat products from smaller farms or ranches, you can be more secure about the health and quality of what you eat while supporting the local economy.

COOKING EQUIPMENT

To cook well, you need to invest in equipment. Even our son has a decent set of knives and pots and pans, and has really enjoyed his adventures in cooking. This list is presented here in order of the most basic to more specialized to respond to your developing abilities and interests. If, for example, you find that you are more interested in baking, you can build on this and treat yourself to some of the many specialty pans. They are beautiful!

THE BASICS FOR NEW COOKS

Apron

Basting brush, silicon

Blender

Can opener

Ceramic baking dishes: rectangular and oval (all ovenproof, varied sizes)

Colander

Corkscrew

Cutting board (I like a heavy wooden board for stability)

Dish towels, tea towels

Dutch oven; enameled cast-iron is the best, and worth it

Flatware, service for 6 (forks, knives, soup spoons, coffee spoons)

Frying pans: 8- and 11-inch nonstick

Garlic press (and here is the commercial: Zyliss is the only way to go)

Half-sheet pans, at least 2 (the most versatile piece of equipment I own)

Hand mixer

Instant-read thermometer

Kitchen shears

Knives: chef's 7- or 8-inch and paring

Measuring cups: American dry-measure and glass liquid-measure

Measuring spoons

Mixing bowls: 1 medium glass and 3 nesting melamine

Oven mitts, pot holders

Parchment paper

Salt cellar

Saucepans with lids: 1- and 3-quart

Sauté pan: 11-inch with lid

Scale for weighing ingredients (especially for baking, where accuracy matters)

Sharpening steel and stone for knives

Spatulas: metal, rubber, silicon

Spoons: large metal, slotted, wooden, silicon

Tongs: traditional locking, nonstick-surface friendly

Vegetable peeler (the serrated ones work best)

NEXT LEVEL—FOR EXPERIENCED COOKS

Cake pans: springform, Bundt

Chef's long tweezers (more precise than tongs)

Food processor (I use this almost daily)

Funnels

Graters: fine and coarse (microplane is far and away the best)

Immersion blender, for making smooth sauces and soups

Knives: boning, an extra paring knife, serrated bread knife

Ladle

Mortar and pestle, aka molcajete

Pepper mill

Pie pan

Rolling pin, wooden-dowel style

Sieves: medium and fine mesh

Spice grinder

Stockpot: 9-quart with lid

Whisks: balloon and flat

Wok

SPECIALTY EQUIPMENT

Banneton (a coiled wooden basket for proofing dough)

Canning equipment: canning jars, jar "lifter," slotted holder for inner lids, canning funnel, and the big splurge—a copper jam pan

Comal, for roasting vegetables and chiles on the stove top

Double boiler, or DIY with a heat-proof measuring cup fitted inside a saucepan

Offset spatula, for spreading frosting and smoothing out batter

Pastry blender, for cutting fat into flours

Pastry cloth, for rolling out dough

Stand mixer, if baking and pasta-making become a big part of your repertoire

Tart pans with removable outer ring, 10- or 15-inch

Tortilla press

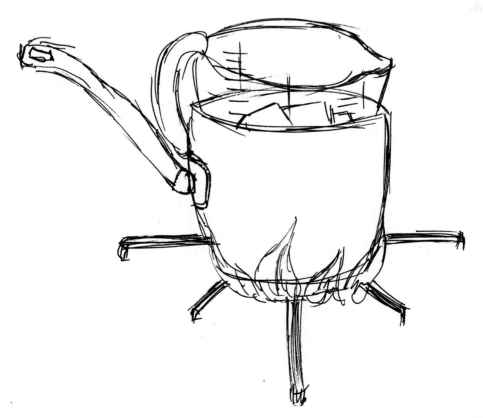

COOKING AND TIMING

It pays to read through a recipe a couple of times to understand the flow of the work. I remember many years ago coming home to my daughter, Nori, and her boyfriend (now husband), Anthony, cooking dinner. They had fried two pork chops to a burnt crisp and were just putting whole potatoes in the oven to bake. Cooking well requires some organization and multitasking, but it is actually a rather relaxing experience. For example, while caramelizing onions for a soup, you can use the wait time to chop other vegetables, heat up your broth, and even set the table.

FOOD SHELF LIFE AND KITCHEN ORGANIZATION

How often do you look in your refrigerator and feel overwhelmed by a wall of food, fresh, not so fresh, leftovers, and take-home boxes from last night's quick meal? Just like a clean desk, an organized refrigerator is inspiring. I rely more on my pantry than my refrigerator for staples such as beans, grains, and canned goods (home canned and purchased) as the basis of most recipes. The fresh additions are simply that and can be picked up easily and quickly. Our refrigerator is usually fairly bare, but it has a generous amount of cheese, ham or sausage, eggs (as these have a long shelf life), homemade jams, and apples, carrots, and beets (the longer-lasting fruits and vegetables). Shorter shelf-life food—fresh meats, leafy vegetables, and tender fruits such as berries—are bought the night before or the same day I plan to use them.

TASTE AS YOU COOK

This extends beyond tasting the dish because you are cooking it; you need to taste ingredients for freshness and for compatibility, too. Undersalting is a new trend based on the fear of high blood pressure. As noted in Kathleen Flinn's terrific book *The Kitchen Counter Cooking School*, only five percent of our recommended salt intake is from home cooking, whereas one can easily exceed healthy salt intake by eating a large serving of packaged ramen in one sitting. And why do chefs use a salt bowl instead of a shaker? So that they can see how much they are using.

FRY THE ONIONS BEFORE THE GARLIC, AND GO SLOWLY

As they cook, onions will darken slowly as they change chemically, caramelizing and becoming sweet tasting. Their texture also changes, from crisp to soft and almost pudding-like. Garlic that cooks too long tastes bitter, so add it toward the end of cooking, and stop cooking as soon as it is softened. Do not wait until it is browned.

BIGGER PIECES OF ANYTHING TAKE LONGER TO COOK

In French cooking, much is written about julienned, diced, and minced ingredients, which simply refers to the size and shape of the cut food (sticks and cubes). There are two reasons for this. One is to better anticipate cooking time; the other is for aesthetics. Knowing this, you can adjust accordingly. You might want something more rustic with larger pieces; just cook longer and add more liquid if necessary.

SWEET POTATOES BAKE MORE QUICKLY THAN WHITE POTATOES

Yes, it's true. And once you begin cooking more, you will begin to recognize which foods are faster finishers. Doneness is also a matter of taste in some cases, safety in others. While al dente is great for pasta, it is unsafe for chicken. It is fine for green beans but terrible for eggplant. Many foods finish cooking in surprising ways. Ceviche, for example, creates a cooked texture in fish through marinating. Parboiled green beans continue to cook when mixed with a vinaigrette. Sweet potatoes, depending on size, usually require only thirty minutes of baking time, whereas white potatoes usually require an hour.

RECIPES REVEAL COOKING PATTERNS

Technique in cooking schools includes knife skills and such cooking terms as dry and wet heat or braising and frying. I break it down a bit more by type of food as well as technique. You will notice there are similarities in how certain dishes are made. Soups almost always start with "first, caramelize the onions." Then there is an addition of chopped vegetables and heated broth, waiting, and then blending, possibly adding a little cream at the end. Once you learn these patterns, you will feel free to try your own ideas, use what's handy, and launch a whole series of recipes. That's how I created many of the recipes in this book.

LEFTOVERS ARE NOT ALWAYS LEFTOVERS

As noted in the Roasted Turkey Breast with Fennel recipe (see page 187), some foods also taste great after the first time you serve them. Think of them as building blocks for other dishes. The leftover turkey breast can be transformed into a Waldorf salad, turkey enchiladas, and, of course, turkey breast sandwiches. The trick is to look at food with imagination. What does it taste like? How would this finished dish work as an ingredient? When our three kids were living at home, this trick was a time- and life-saver. I often slow-roasted an extra-large pork butt on Sunday, and it reappeared throughout the week in various transformations without the word leftovers passing from anyone's lips.

SOME EXAMPLES

MASHED POTATOES: For a hearty breakfast the next morning, mix in a bit of grated parmesan and possibly a bit of kosher salt, and form into patties. Fry in butter until crispy and brown on each side. Serve with a fried egg for a hearty breakfast.

ROASTED PORK BUTT: Shred and pile into corn tortillas with a salsa for soft tacos.

RICE PILAF: Add cooked rice to soups for added texture. Our kids loved something called Cheesy Rice. They heated rice pilaf with grated cheese (whatever was around) in the toaster oven or microwave. Sometimes they added toasted nuts to the mess. It was amazingly good comfort food.

PLAIN RICE: The basis of rice pudding, cooked rice adds heft to vegetable casseroles, such as Vegetable Tian (see page 164).

COOKED GRAINS, SUCH AS QUINOA OR BARLEY: Repurpose with a strongly flavored vinaigrette, a generous amount of chopped flat-leaf parsley, and chopped tomatoes for a delicious salad. Add crumbled feta and you've got a complete meal. See also Three Salades Composées (see page 148).

COOKED BEETS: Dice and add a flavored vinaigrette, a few crumbles of goat cheese, and chopped toasted walnuts.

"BATCH PROCESS"

When Eric and I were dating and he was a single dad, his favorite term about anything that had to do with housekeeping was "batch processing," which included washing the dishes and similar tidying-up chores.

While not entirely agreeing, I did fall into a rhythm of cooking certain foods ahead of time on the weekends and then finishing them throughout the week. Such tasks included grating cheeses, toasting nuts, baking sweet potatoes, making chicken broth and freezing some of it, starting crème fraîche or other sauces, pickling cucumbers or mushrooms, mixing yogurt or ricotta herbed cheese, and soaking and cooking beans. This preparation extends to all fresh foods upon purchase. I take time to wash and dry all lettuce and other soft-leaf vegetables before putting them away. During the week, when I came home after a long day, these inspiring "ready-made" ingredients made dinner easy and creative and provided some very healthy snacking for the kids.

WHY LET MEAT REST?

Roasts of beef, pork, lamb, and whole chicken should be allowed to rest 15 to 20 minutes after being removed from the oven so that the meat can finish cooking (internal temperature will go up another five degrees) and so the juices will reabsorb into the meat. A roast that is carved immediately will lose a great deal of its internal moisture.

HOMEMADE IS NOT ALWAYS BEST

This seems sacrilegious, but there are certain ingredients that really are too complex and fussy for most of us and can, in fact, discourage us from home cooking. I buy pizza dough already made from a number of sources, phyllo dough from various Armenian markets, pasta, and good-quality mayonnaise and mustards. However, when feeling ambitious and time allows, by all means try anything. Eric once tried croissants—he never did this again.

YOU DON'T HAVE TO COOK VEGETABLES AT THE LAST MINUTE

We all have memories of gray-green beans, overcooked and mushy, from long-ago family dinners. To make good-tasting vegetables without last-minute stress, throw them into boiling salted water, cook until their color heightens—bright green for green beans, for example. Drain and immediately cool in a bowl of ice water. Once cooled, remove them with a slotted spoon, dry completely with a towel, and save them until mealtime to heat in a sauté pan with warm, foamy butter, salt, and herbs or spices.

Roasting is another way to cook vegetables without stress. Cut thick slices of root vegetables (carrots, parsnips, beets, onions, or potatoes), mix with a coating of olive oil and salt, and spread over a parchment-lined half-sheet pan. Bake until done—a bit caramelized and browned—for 35 to 45 minutes in a hot oven (about 400°). Another great way to cook vegetables without fussing is to cut carrots, turnips, onions, and potatoes into quarters and place under a chicken for roasting. They act as a rack for the chicken, which flavors the meat. I love symbiosis.

AND LAST, BUT NOT LEAST, USE YOUR SENSES AS WELL AS TIME TO KNOW WHEN FOOD IS "DONE"

Ovens vary in temperature; the freshness of vegetables can change cooking times; a hot day can mean a faster rise for bread. Trust your eyes, nose, and touch when cooking—not just the timer.

"If the plate is a canvas, ingredients are like paints to me. I seek, I mix, I match, I make companions of enemies. Delivering a thought- and soul-provoking canvas is always my goal. I make complicated things look easy and easy things interesting." Minh Phan, with a basket of inspiring ingredients gathered from a favorite community garden in Pasadena.

PROFILE: MINH PHAN

Minh is a committed outlier, someone who has straddled cultures, communities, geographies, and a carefully balanced space between business expertise and idealism. She came to this country as a one-year-old, leaving South Vietnam with her father, a member of the South Vietnamese navy, and her mother, then twenty-four. Her father's prescience about the South's changing political fortunes ensured that the Phan family was safe and settled in Wisconsin immediately after the fall of Saigon. The leave-taking was dramatic, with little time to pack or say good-bye.

Wisconsin's food culture of brats and beer may be the diametric opposite of Vietnamese food, known for its complexity, refinement, and intense flavors. Both parents worked, and the various bits and pieces foraged from the refrigerator gave their preteen latchkey daughter even more license to experiment with unlikely food pairings—an experience that served Minh well as a chef in later years.

Minh describes her mother, Lanh, as a phenomenal cook, managing a full menu of exquisite food every night even after a full day at work. For Vietnamese families, this means five elements: rice, soup, stir-fry, braised protein, and a vegetable that is boiled, pickled, or raw. A favorite food included the simplest—a porridge after Thanksgiving, inspired by the richness of a broth from the turkey carcass or ham bone.

After a career in marketing, Minh attended the California School of Culinary Arts and the New School of Cooking in Southern California. She trained in some of New York's finest restaurants, admiring the exacting requirements of technique but despairing over the waste of so much good food. Despite nearly twenty years in her profession, she remains an intentional learner. Her nomadic forays into pop-up kitchens through a network of colleagues' restaurants have contributed to the ongoing innovation of her cooking.

A return to Vietnam revealed the diversity of its food culture, based in part on geographic location. The north is more austere; its ingredients are of high quality but limited in quantity and variety due to climate. Central Vietnam was home to the last imperial family, with its food reflecting the elegant small bites of ancient Vietnamese royal cuisine. And South Vietnam has a more gregarious food scene, with layers of flavors and a greater variety of ingredients, as its growing season is much longer than that of other parts of the country.

At porridge + puffs, her restaurant in Historic Filipinotown, Minh has turned her prodigious energy and inventiveness toward two of the world cuisine's simplest and most universal food types: porridges and fried bread, or puffs. Each element of a porridge—the broth, the rice, the aromatics, the proteins, and the vegetables—gives her license to draw upon her wide-ranging food heritage and experience. It is a freeing form of experimentation, whose structure is based on technique, an unusually sensitive palate, and interchangeable, carefully crafted pantry ingredients. Her refrigerator-foraging instincts as a young child now find expression in urban gardens, where the produce acts as inspiration. Have you ever tasted the yellow flower buds of fennel? Trust me, they are as Minh describes: "heavenly candy."

Braised tofu with pickles
A childhood favorite prepared by her mother, Lahn, Minh's first cooking inspiration.

Tuna and rice
A typical lunch food pairing that embarrassed young Minh in Wisconsin, far from her Vietnamese roots.

Koda Farms Rice
High-quality, heirloom rice; a key ingredient in Minh's porridge dishes.

Geranium Pickled Baby Onions
An example of Minh's sensitive and adventurous palate (see page 51).

Amaranth
A weed transformed into glorious food—amaranth or citrus tempura.

Lemongrass, shallots, and ginger
Minh's Asian mirepoix, an essential flavoring.

Proof Bakery in Atwater
Proof, owned by friend and collaborator Na Young Ma; site of a Minh pop-up kitchen.

Farmer Mai
Described by Minh as truly inspirational and "the future of farming"; grows heirloom, ethnic crops using sustainable and drought-tolerant methods.

Nasturtium + fennel + cherries + tangerines
One of Minh's sources for quality food foraging is the Hollywood Farmers' Market, home of her late, great café, Field Trip.

Edible flowers
More creative food ingredients and flavors. Mustard flowers are a favorite—spicy and beautiful.

Stock
A carefully prepared stock is the foundation of a delicious porridge.

Porridge
A signature dish, which Minh has redefined as fine cuisine.

Puffs
Light, crispy, airy pastry, another of Minh's signature dishes.

The Basics

FOR THE NEW COOK

I learned to cook by watching skilled home cooks. I have never forgotten a long-ago Thanksgiving when my husband's Aunt Beanie matter-of-factly began her turkey gravy by simply placing the roasting pan directly on the stove's burners. Or when I saw a friend's mother start her hard-boiled eggs in cold water. Or when a French friend of mine showed me how to clean mussels. Without these friendly guides, so much of cooking becomes the purview of the expert, the supremely trained chef. This book does not assume or require mastery; instead, it invites you to learn, to be inspired, and hopefully to continue on your own cooking journey.

HOW TO CARE FOR KNIVES

It is worth investing in a good set of knives. If you care for them, they will last a lifetime. Quality stainless steel knives are made so that the blade continues through the length of the handle. Another indication of quality is blades made of multilayered steel. A sharp knife is a pleasure to use. Knives need to be sharpened regularly, either by you or a professional sharpener. You will sharpen them more frequently if you can do this in your own kitchen. Acquire a two-grit diamond stone, 600 on one side and 1200 on the other. Push the blade edge down the length of the stone, beginning with the 600 grit. Hold the blade fairly flat (about ten degrees). You should be able to slip three quarters under the highest point of the back of the blade. Do your best to hold this angle to avoid rocking back and forth as you grind off the edge. Switch over to the fine 1200 grit, using the same motions but maintaining a slightly higher angle (four quarters instead of three). In both stages, you must press hard enough so that you are grinding away metal. You should feel the bite of the stone as it removes metal from the edge of the knife. You will know it is sharp when you delicately place the edge of the knife on your thumbnail and it catches instantly. A sharp edge has matching angles on each side. A sharpening steel acts as a repair mechanism between sharpenings by straightening the edge of the blade. It does not sharpen edges. It is a long, thin tool, cylindrical in shape, that comes with good-quality knife sets. Knives should be hand washed, dried immediately after use, and stored in a slotted countertop or drawer holder. Never put knives in a dishwasher.

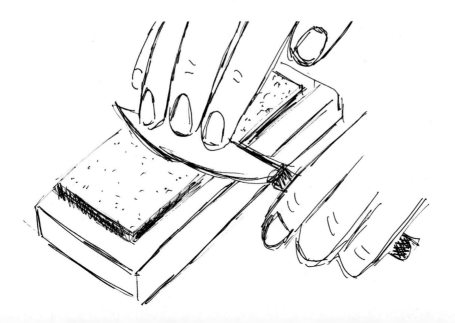

HOW TO CUT MEAT AGAINST THE GRAIN

Roasts are basically muscle and thus have a grain to them. Most cuts are muscle that runs up and down the leg or along the backbone of the animal. Therefore, in order to serve tender, easily cut slices, it is necessary to cut across the grain of the muscle fiber. If the roast is on the tough side, then cut thinner slices. Fibers are tough, so shorter segments will be easier to chew. Thin or thick, presentable slices of even thickness require a sharp carving knife, preferably one with a long, straight, thin blade.

HOW TO CARVE FOWL

Begin by placing fowl breast-side up on the carving board. Carving fowl, whether a chicken, turkey, or something more unusual, begins with identifying the joints. For a large fowl such as a turkey, the breasts and thighs may be carved into slices as well. Unlike beef roasts, slicing fowl is always done *with* the grain.

Loosen the legs by cutting the skin between the thigh and the breast with the knife tip. Pull the thighs away from the breast toward the cutting board. Find the joint where the thighbone attaches to the carcass and cut straight down to remove the whole leg. Repeat with the other leg. Then wiggle each leg to find the joint between the thigh and the drumstick. Cut straight down on that joint and place those pieces on your serving platter. Repeat with second leg.

To remove the breasts from the carcass, cut down on either side of the breastbone until you feel the resistance of the cartilage beneath. Using that cartilage as your guide, run your knife down either side of the bird until the breast is separated. Do the same on the other side. Place breasts on the cutting board, skin-side up, and pull wings outward. Cut down at the second joint. Transfer wings to serving platter as is, or remove the wing tips by cutting at the joint. Serve breasts whole, cut each into two pieces, or slice and fan meat out. Dispose of the carcass or simmer it to make your own broth (see pages 34 and 35).

Some of my favorite and most-used cooking tools: sharpened knives, cook's tweezers (great for frying), and my brother-in-law's beautiful handmade wooden spatulas.

HOW TO COOK PASTA

5 to 6 servings

INGREDIENTS
1 tablespoon salt
1 pound pasta (any kind)

METHOD
– In a large pot that can hold at least 3 quarts of water, heat water on high until a rolling boil is reached.

– Add salt and pasta.

– Quickly stir, making sure the water covers pasta and all pieces are separated.

– Reduce heat, but maintain a low boil.

– Cook, uncovered, according to package directions.

– Test for al dente (not crunchy, but not mushy; the pasta should have a bit of a bite to it).

– Drain in a colander, reserving a small amount of cooking liquid in the pot.

– Do not rinse with water—you want to keep the starch that has accumulated on the pasta; it will help thicken the sauce you will add later.

– Return pasta to the cooking pot with the small amount of water.

– Add butter or any warmed sauce you wish.

FOOD SOURCES: Until now, I could not find even a close second for the taste of homemade pasta, and then I tried Semolina Artisanal Pasta in Pasadena, a little store-front pasta-making enterprise where we retail customers can enter, buy, and swoon. This pasta is a whole different animal; it has texture and taste, and holds its chewiness. Otherwise, Eagle Rock Italian Bakery and Deli and Roma Italian Deli and Grocery have found a sweet spot between good-quality flour, variety, and value.

HOW TO COOK LONG-GRAIN RICE

Rice inspires strong preferences among rice-eating cultures, suggesting the great, wide world of variety beyond this very basic recipe. Short-grain Cal Rose, long-grain basmati and jasmine, the tiny Kala Jeera, and carnaroli or arborio, a foundation for risotto, are just a few examples. Shorter-grain rice contains more starch, which becomes almost creamy when cooked slowly. This recipe works for long-grain basmati or jasmine, and produces fluffy, drier rice with separate grains.

Makes 2 cups

INGREDIENTS
1 cup white long-grain rice
1⅓ cups water

METHOD

– Wash the starch from the rice. Start by placing the rice in a large bowl; fill the bowl with cold water and swirl the grains through your fingers. Tip out the starchy water, making sure the rice is held back, and repeat until the water runs clear. I use a sieve for the last rinse to make sure as much water as possible is drained.

– Combine rice and 1⅓ cups water in a pot large enough for the rice to double in volume as it cooks. A good rule of thumb is that rice and water are no higher than halfway up the pot.

– Bring water to a hard boil over high heat. Stir with a wooden spoon, making sure that no grains stick to the bottom of the pot. Turn the heat down to low, cover the pot, and continue cooking for 15 minutes. Turn the heat off and let the rice rest for an additional 10 to 15 minutes. If the rice is still a bit too moist, remove the cover and let sit a few minutes longer.

FOOD SOURCES: To experiment with rice varieties, try markets that cater to rice-eating cultures, such as Bhanu Indian Grocery and Cuisine and H Mart. Claro's Italian Markets, Eagle Rock Italian Bakery and Deli, and Roma Italian Deli and Grocery carry rice that is ideal for risotto. Cookbook and Marukai Market feature Koda Farms Heirloom Rice. This rice is a revelation; it has a delicate perfume and a sturdy texture, even when used for porridges and risottos.

HOW TO POACH EGGS

With wisdom and contributions from Doug Herman.

INGREDIENTS

1 or 2 eggs per serving

1 tablespoon white vinegar

METHOD

– Fill a medium nonstick, fairly deep skillet or saucepan three-quarters full with water. Add vinegar.

– Heat until barely simmering. Crack the eggs into a small bowl, one at a time, and then slide each egg into the simmering water.

– Cook for a few minutes. As the egg whites start to become opaque, begin ladling the hot water over the top of the eggs.

– Cook slowly, ladling carefully to ensure that the tops of the eggs are not undercooked.

– Cook until the egg yolks begin to become slightly firm and then carefully, one at a time, remove the eggs with a slotted spoon to a folded-over paper towel.

– Carefully pick up the paper towel and flip the egg over onto a piece of buttered toast or onto the prepared tortilla and beans of Sunday Quesadillas (see page 99).

FOOD SOURCE: Okay, I am saying it: Fresh, organic eggs, raised humanely, taste better and are worth the difference in cost. What am I talking about? Twenty-five cents versus fifty or seventy-five cents per egg. Pasture-raised eggs are delicious, because the eggs are fresher and the hens manage their own diet of mostly grubs and grass. I love the almost saffron yolks and the firmer whites. Try your local farmers' market, and don't be afraid to ask about what their chickens eat and where they hang out. Culture Club 101 and Cookbook both carry high-quality eggs. You can find pasture-raised eggs at your local supermarket, but check the date of expiration on the carton. The more days left before expiration, the fresher the eggs.

HOW TO MAKE GREAT CHICKEN OR TURKEY BROTH FROM LEFTOVERS

Best after roasting a large chicken or a turkey. Use in Vegetable Soup—One Recipe, Ten Versions (see page 116) or any other soup recipe.

Makes 1 to 3 quarts, depending on poultry size

INGREDIENTS

Roasted carcass of a large chicken or small turkey
1 raw onion, peeled and studded with 3 to 4 cloves
2 raw carrots, peeled and cut into 3 large pieces per carrot
Salt and pepper, to taste

METHOD

– Place roasted turkey or chicken carcass in a soup pot; cover with cold water.

– Add onion and carrot.

– Heat mixture until boiling. Reduce to simmer.

– After 5 to 6 hours, strain the broth through a sieve.

– Throw away the carcass and vegetables.

– Add salt and pepper, to taste.

– Pour the broth into a large bowl.

– Cool for about 30 minutes, then cover broth with plastic wrap and place in the refrigerator overnight.

– Skim off all fat.

– Pour broth into storage containers. Best to store in freezer unless you are going to use immediately.

NOTE: Diehards freeze the chicken fat to use in a number of rich dishes, including pâtés, chopped liver, and as the fat for roasted potatoes.

HOW TO MAKE CHICKEN BROTH THE EASY WAY

Makes 3 quarts

INGREDIENTS

6 pounds chicken necks and backs

METHOD

– Cover chicken with cold water in a large 6-quart soup pot.

– Heat water to boiling.

– Lower the heat to a simmer and cook for 4 to 6 hours or more (I usually simmer the broth all night).

– Drain broth through a sieve and capture it in a large bowl.

– Cool for about 30 minutes, then cover the broth with plastic wrap and place in the refrigerator.

– Remove layer of fat. (See Note facing page.)

– Ladle broth into freezer containers, label, and freeze. Use as needed.

NOTE: This broth is made without salt, allowing for a neutral flavor for the most versatility in cooking. I add salt and other seasonings to the broth, depending on the requirements of the dish.

FOOD SOURCE: Fish King sells more than just fish—chicken parts, too!

Experienced cooks are organized. This not only means they collect and measure ingredients for a dish before beginning to cook, it also means taking a bit of time to invest in making what I call pantry superchargers. These are homemade ingredients that add much to the flavor of a dish without a great deal of work. These pantry superchargers have a reasonable shelf or refrigerator life, so they are available as an addition or substitution for a great many dishes. I have included some suggestions for their use throughout the cookbook. See *Try This* notes, but don't hesitate to experiment on your own.

CLARIFIED BUTTER

To clarify butter, place 1 pound of good-quality unsalted butter in a heavy-bottomed saucepan. Cook over low heat until the butter is melted. It will separate into a bright yellow liquid and white foam. Remove from heat. With a large spoon, carefully remove the foam and discard. Pour the bright yellow liquid into a storage jar and use whenever you are cooking with butter. If you want to be thorough, pour the liquid through a fine sieve lined with several layers of cheesecloth. Store in the refrigerator. Clarified butter does not smoke or burn nearly as easily as untreated butter. It is also called *ghee* and is a consistent ingredient in Indian cooking.

FOOD SOURCE: Armen Market in Pasadena sells solid blocks of Challenge Butter called "chef's cut" at a very reasonable price, usually less than four dollars a pound. I don't see any reason to pay extra for wrapped sections of butter.

YOGURT CHEESE AND RICOTTA CHEESE SPREADS

Yogurt Cheese and Ricotta Cheese Spreads make a great foundation for lowfat cheese spreads. Just add your favorite seasonings, such as fresh herbs with garlic or spicy roasted chiles.

YOGURT CHEESE

Makes 2 cups

INGREDIENTS

2 cups lowfat or full-fat plain yogurt or Greek yogurt
Handful delicately flavored herbs, minced (chives, mint, basil, tarragon—you choose)
Up to 1 tablespoon kosher salt, to taste

METHOD

– Pour yogurt into a cheesecloth-draped colander or sieve that is sitting in a large bowl. If using Greek yogurt, skip this step and go straight to the herbs and salt.

– Place in refrigerator overnight. Whey (the liquid) will separate from curds (the solid).

– Add the herbs to the yogurt and stir until just combined.

– Add salt sparingly and taste after each addition. Store in the refrigerator, in a covered jar, up to 3 weeks.

RICOTTA CHEESE SPREAD

Great on Crostini (see page 61)

Makes 2 cups

INGREDIENTS

About 2 cups good-quality whole-milk ricotta cheese from an Italian deli
3 to 4 tablespoons minced fresh herbs, such as flat-leaf parsley, basil, chives, and thyme
Kosher salt, to taste

METHOD

– Mix together ricotta cheese and herbs. Add salt sparingly, tasting after each addition.

– Store in the refrigerator, in a covered jar, up to 1 week.

FOOD SOURCES: Cookbook, Eagle Rock Italian Bakery and Deli, Roma Italian Deli and Grocery.

CRÈME FRAÎCHE

This is an ingredient you will want to have around. It is easy to make, delicious, and much less expensive than the purchased version. I use it on nearly everything that tastes better with a creamy tang; it is yummier than store-bought sour cream, as its texture and flavor are more delicate.

Makes 2 cups

INGREDIENTS

2 cups heavy cream (avoid the ultra-pasteurized version, as it may never thicken and has a lot of the nutritional quality blasted out of it)
½ cup buttermilk

METHOD

– In a tall pitcher or other large container, whisk together cream and buttermilk until incorporated.

– Cover container with a light cloth or a couple layers of cheesecloth and leave at room temperature. The mixture will thicken within 1 to 2 days, depending on the room's temperature, often only 1.

– Before using, give the crème fraîche a good whisk.

– Store in the refrigerator, covered, up to 2 weeks.

FOOD SOURCES: Great dairy products are becoming more and more available. Try Cookbook or Sprouts Farmers Market for a variety of good dairy choices. Straus Family Creamery is one example of a resource for high-quality milk and cream.

AGHOIAN FAMILY YOGURT

This particular version of yogurt is the simplest I have ever encountered—and it is delicious, too. Jack Aghoian's family's yogurt starter began generations ago; you can start yours today! (See Jack's profile on page 139.) As in most cooking, the ingredients make a difference. Use good-quality whole milk and yogurt for your starter. When purchasing yogurt for your first batch, avoid yogurt with added ingredients, and avoid ultra-pasteurized milk, as the high-heat process can kill some of the enzymes that create yogurt and can affect the milk's nutrients as well.

Makes 2 quarts

INGREDIENTS

2 quarts whole pasteurized milk
2 to 3 tablespoons whole-milk plain yogurt (to be used as a starter)

METHOD

– Heat milk in a generous-size, heavy-bottomed cooking pot over low heat until frothy. Continue cooking until the milk "rises." Do not let the milk boil. Milk temperature will be about 180°.

– Remove the steamed milk from heat and allow it to cool to 115° to 120°. One way to cool the milk a bit more quickly is to pour it into a bowl. Cooling takes longer than you might expect.

– In a small bowl, combine yogurt with 1 cup warmed milk to equalize the temperature.

– Add yogurt mixture to remaining warm milk and stir until incorporated.

– Cover the pot or bowl with a lid or plate, then wrap with a towel to hold in the warmth, and place in a warm, draft-free spot. Jack places his yogurt on top of his O'Keefe and Merritt stove, where the burners are warmed by a pilot light. Jack's mother, Mary, just wraps her yogurt in a towel and places it in the oven. There is no pilot light to maintain warmth, but it is draft-free. I use a simple yogurt maker, which is basically a single-temperature slow cooker. In this case, the milk and yogurt mixture is transferred to the bowl of the yogurt maker.

– Yogurt is ready in 4 hours; longer if you prefer a bit more tang.

– Reserve ½ cup yogurt to start your next batch. It will keep, covered, in the refrigerator for up to 2 weeks.

TRY THIS: Jack suggests a number of ways to enjoy yogurt. Add a dollop on a puréed soup for tang and presentation. Prepare a simple salad by dicing a half dozen Persian cucumbers and adding a tablespoon or so of yogurt, a minced garlic clove, a pinch or two of dried, crumbled mint leaves, and salt to taste. Or use your homemade yogurt as a base for fruit lassis and smoothies.

FOOD SOURCES: Garni Meat Market has excellent homemade yogurt, which could be used as a superior starter. Cookbook, Culture Club 101, Sprouts Farmers Market, and many farmers' markets sell high-quality milk and yogurt products.

PESTO THREE WAYS

Pesto is one of the most flexible of recipes, relying on a combination of nuts or seeds, oil, fresh herbs, salt, and garlic. Classic and Country-Style Pesto are delicious on sliced tomatoes, on buttered pasta, spread on crostini, or as a flavorful addition to a sandwich.

Each recipe makes about 1½ cups

CLASSIC PESTO

INGREDIENTS

1 cup pine nuts (taste to make sure they are fresh)
¼ cup good-quality olive oil
2 generous bunches basil leaves, about 1 ½ cups (remove the stems, as they are bitter)
1 large clove garlic, pressed
Kosher salt, to taste

METHOD

– Blend the first 4 ingredients in a food processor or blender. Add a scant teaspoon of kosher salt and taste, adding more if necessary. Blend again until the pesto is very smooth.

– Pesto keeps up to 2 days, covered, in the refrigerator.

COUNTRY-STYLE PESTO

Substitute walnuts for pine nuts. Blend all ingredients until coarsely chopped.

CILANTRO PESTO

I like to serve this as an appetizer with tostados, or mixed into hot, buttered soba noodles.

INGREDIENTS

2 cups chopped cilantro, leaves only for a smoother texture
⅓ cup safflower or vegetable oil
⅓ cup toasted pepitas (pumpkin seeds)
2 tablespoons fresh lime juice
1 clove garlic
¼ teaspoon salt (the cotija cheese is salty already, so you may choose to omit the salt)
2 jalapeños, with or without seeds, depending on desired heat level (optional)
2 to 4 tablespoons grated cotija cheese

METHOD

– Combine all ingredients but the cheese in a food processor. Add 2 tablespoons cheese and blend. Add up to 2 tablespoons more cheese, depending on your preference.

FOOD SOURCES: Pesto will taste good only if the ingredients are high quality and fresh. Try Aladdin Nuthouse for nuts; farmers' markets for herbs and olive oil; Nicole's Market & Café for olive oil; La Mayordomia Market, Super A Foods, and Vallarta Supermarkets for pepita seeds, cheese, and tostados.

MARIO MAKES SALSA

I think it must be all of the faux salsas I have been exposed to in my life that made Mario Rodriguez's version a revelation. Please don't chuckle, those of you who grew up eating the real deal. Its simplicity and versatility is the genius of this salsa. (See Mario's profile on page 103.)

Makes about 1 cup

INGREDIENTS
6 jalapeños, whole
2 medium cloves garlic, unpeeled
1 medium tomato, whole
1 teaspoon, or more salt to taste

METHOD
– On a comal or in a medium, heavy-bottomed frying pan—cast-iron works well— roast jalapeños, garlic, and tomato over medium high heat. Turn the vegetables occasionally until softened and blackened in a few places. This takes a bit of time but little attention.

– Remove the vegetables from the pan; place them in a plastic or paper bag and close the bag.

– When the vegetables have cooled, remove them from the bag and peel them. Wear gloves, as the capsaicin oil in the jalapeños can burn.

– Though Mario's mom, Lupe, taught him to peel the vegetables, you can also leave them as is, without peeling—with the exception of the garlic, which is always peeled.

– For the traditional method of blending, add the peeled garlic cloves to a mortar and pestle, or molcajete, and mash until they turn into a paste.

– Add the tomatoes and continue mashing; then add 1 jalapeño at a time until all of the vegetables are incorporated.

– Add salt and mix with a spoon. Taste, and add more salt if desired.

– For a smoother texture, use a blender in place of a mortar and pestle, and blend until smooth. Mario uses a blender to save time when making a large amount of salsa.

– Pour salsa into a glass container and store in the refrigerator, covered, for up to 3 days.

NOTE: This salsa is hot; if you can't stand heat, remove some or all of the seeds from the jalapeños. These chiles vary in heat level; chiles with striations on the surface are especially hot. I recommend a quick taste after each jalapeño addition.

TRY THIS: Salsa makes a fine side sauce for scrambled eggs or tamales and is a key ingredient for huevos rancheros.

FOOD SOURCES: El Mercado de Los Angeles, La Princesita Carnicera y Tortilleria, Super A Foods, Super King Market, Vallarta Supermarkets.

SIMPLE SYRUP

I make simple syrup for a number of purposes, including canning fruit (such as Tart Pie Cherries, see page 77) and as a base for sodas. An interesting variation is the herbal simple syrup, below. Simple syrup is also a more elegant way to sweeten hot or iced tea.

THIN (FOR CANNING)

2 cups sugar to 4 cups water. Stir well before heating and bring slowly to a boil. Continue to boil for about 10 minutes, until the sugar is completely dissolved.

MEDIUM (FOR CANNING AND FLAVORING SOFT DRINKS)

3 cups sugar to 4 cups water. Prepare as for thin syrup.

HEAVY (FOR DESSERTS)

4½ cups sugar to 4 cups water. Dissolve and stir very carefully to prevent crystallization and scorching.

FLAVORED SYRUP FOR HOMEMADE SODAS AND LOVELY TEA

Use medium simple syrup as the base.

Herbs for a delicious summer drink: Take a large handful of fresh herbs, such as basil, thyme, and mint—or whatever you have in the garden. Sage and rosemary should be used in moderation, as these are quite strong. Add to the hot syrup and simmer for about 10 minutes, until the scent of herbs is obvious.

Ginger for a refreshing soda or hot tea: Peel and dice 1 large piece of ginger (about ¼ pound); add to medium simple syrup. Boil, then reduce heat and cook over medium heat for about 15 minutes.

Orange for a delicious soda: Zest 2 medium oranges and add to the syrup, along with juice squeezed from the oranges. Cook 10 more minutes. Let cool. It is great as a sweetener for iced tea or with soda water for a light orange soda.

To finish all syrup flavors: Pour mixture through a fine-mesh sieve, reserving the syrup and discarding the solids. Pour the flavored syrup into a tightly covered bottle and store in the refrigerator.

To make an herbal, ginger, or orange soda: Pour 1 tablespoon or more syrup into the bottom of a tall drinking glass. Add a few inches of bubbly water and stir. Add ice cubes and pour additional bubbly water until the glass is nearly full. Stir again.

To make ginger tea: Add 1 tablespoon or more ginger syrup to a mug. Pour in barely boiling water and stir.

EVERYDAY VINAIGRETTE

Great on butter lettuce or other soft lettuce. Sherry vinegar is often from Spain and can be purchased in most quality markets.

Makes about ¾ cup

INGREDIENTS

½ cup extra-virgin olive oil
¼ cup or more vinegar (my favorite is a good-quality sherry vinegar)
Large pinch kosher salt
Several grinds black pepper
Small pinch sugar
2 to 3 cloves garlic—use garlic press or mince very finely
1 teaspoon Dijon mustard

METHOD

– Combine all ingredients and whisk until thickened.

– Taste and adjust for seasoning; add more oil if too vinegary.

– Serve at room temperature but store in the refrigerator.

TRY THIS: A delicious variation of Everyday Vinaigrette requires just a few ingredient substitutions. For a lighter version, replace olive oil with ¼ cup olive oil and ¼ cup grapeseed oil. Replace the Dijon mustard with the juice of half a blood orange. Replace the sherry vinegar with ¼ cup balsamic vinegar (avoid the aged syrupy version). Add 2 additional cloves garlic, pressed or finely minced. Mix all ingredients but the oil together and taste. Drizzle the oil in while mixing; this will help the mixture emulsify for a thicker dressing. The dressing should be very garlicky with a sweet undertone.

FOOD SOURCES: Extra-virgin olive oil means it is unrefined; that is, produced without chemicals (a good thing!). Look for oil that is packaged in glass bottles, which prevents chemicals from leaching into the oil. First press means nothing, as there is no second press, but check the pressing or packaging date for freshness. California-produced olive oils score well on comparative taste tests, so try your farmers' market producers. Now, for vinegars: a confusing array if there ever was one. I change up my vinegars depending on the type of salad made; they last indefinitely, so it is reasonable to have several types on hand. Frequently used vinegars for salads are sherry or champagne vinegar, which offer a bit of sweetness to vinegar's tang. Nicole's Market & Café and Surfas Culinary District carry a good selection of vinegars and olive oils. And last but not least is honey. For a real education, visit Victor Jaramillo, "the oldest beekeeper in the country." He sells gorgeous honey made from his hives in El Sereno (see page 231).

WALNUT OR HAZELNUT DRESSING

Best used for "sweet" salads, such as mixed greens, dried cranberries, and goat cheese.

Makes ¾ cup dressing

INGREDIENTS

¼ cup hazelnuts or walnuts, toasted
½ cup grapeseed oil (if using hazelnuts, hazelnut oil adds great flavor)
¼ cup champagne or sherry vinegar
2 cloves garlic, pressed
1 tablespoon honey
Large pinch kosher salt
½ teaspoon Dijon mustard

METHOD

– Place hazelnuts or walnuts in large mortar and pestle and mash.

– Add oil, vinegar, garlic, honey, salt, and mustard and whisk until thickened.

BLUE CHEESE SALAD DRESSING

Best on romaine lettuce with ripe tomatoes; it is excellent with additional crumbles of blue cheese.

Makes about 2 cups

INGREDIENTS

4 ounces Roquefort or Maytag blue cheese, chopped or crumbled
1 cup mayonnaise
1 cup heavy cream or ½ cup plain Greek yogurt
2 tablespoons apple cider vinegar or 1 tablespoon freshly squeezed lemon juice
1 teaspoon kosher salt
½ teaspoon freshly ground pepper

METHOD

– Place Roquefort or blue cheese, mayonnaise, cream or yogurt, vinegar or lemon juice, salt, and pepper in a medium bowl.

– Mash with a fork until relatively smooth. Store in a covered jar in the refrigerator. For chunkier dressing, reserve a third of the cheese, break into small chunks, and add after mixing.

FOOD SOURCE: It is not necessary to purchase expensive Roquefort or blue cheese for this recipe. I often go to Armen Market for their gorgonzola.

A SAMPLING OF MINH'S PANTRY ESSENTIALS

Minh Phan's beautiful food usually starts with a base, such as her signature porridges, whose subtle taste allows for the addition of more intense flavors that come from personally crafted pantry items. Her judicious and informed use of simple-to-make ingredients yields unique and complex flavors. I have found that these ingredients serve as a kit of parts, interchangeable and applicable to my own food as well.

MINH'S NEGI OIL

Makes approximately 1 cup

INGREDIENTS

1 bunch Negi (Japanese onions) or green onions, finely sliced, green sections separated from white
1 cup grapeseed oil, divided

METHOD

– Place the white sections of the onions in a medium heat-proof bowl.

– In a small pan over a medium flame, heat ¾ cup oil.

– When the oil is hot (around 350°), remove pan from heat and add the remaining ¼ cup oil. The temperature of the oil will reduce to about 250°.

– Pour the oil over the white onion slices; let stand for 1 minute.

– Add the green sections of the onions.

– Cover the bowl and let onions steep at room temperature for 24 hours.

– Strain the oil into a pourable container, discarding the onions.

– Store Negi Oil, covered, in the refrigerator, for use as needed. It will last up to 2 weeks.

MINH'S MAKRUT COMPOUND BUTTER

Makes an 8-ounce roll or a small bowl

INGREDIENTS

⅓ cup cream
Salt to taste (Minh suggests Jacobsen's salt)
12 to 15 makrut leaves, washed, dried, and sliced into thin strips
Zest of 1 makrut lime (optional, as it is hard to find the limes for purchase)
1 cup (2 sticks) unsalted butter, softened

METHOD

– Place cream and 1 or 2 pinches of salt in a 3-quart saucepan. Add the makrut leaves and steep over low heat for 5 to 10 minutes.

– Let mixture cool; remove makrut leaves, reserving a few strips if you don't have zest.

– Mash cream and a pinch more salt into butter. Add zest, if available, or makrut strips.

– Place butter mixture on an 8-inch square of parchment paper, form into a roll, and twist the ends shut, or press mixture into a small bowl.

– Keep makrut butter in the refrigerator, covered, for up to 2 weeks.

Minh Phan's "mise en place": shallots, ginger, lemongrass, habanero chiles, fennel fronds, and amaranth, used for dishes such as Vegan Porridge (see page 130) and her other imaginative recipes.

MINH'S GERANIUM PICKLED BABY ONIONS

These are not only delicious, but absolutely beautiful, resembling tiny rose petals on a plate.

Makes 1 cup

INGREDIENTS

1 cup rice vinegar
¼ cup sugar
Pinch salt
1/2 cup water
½ cup rose geranium leaves, packed
¼ pound baby red pearl onions, outer skin peeled, and cut in half

METHOD

– In a 3-quart saucepan over high heat, stir rice vinegar, sugar, salt, and 1/2 cup water until sugar and salt are dissolved.

– Place geranium leaves in the bottom of a clean 16-ounce glass jar.

– Add onions, then pour hot vinegar mixture over onions and geranium leaves.

– The onions will become flavorful within 3 to 4 hours. Keep in the refrigerator, covered, up to 4 weeks.

MINH'S HABANERO AND KUMQUAT SALT

When prepping hot chiles such as habaneros, it is necessary to wear gloves.

Makes 1 cup

INGREDIENTS

10 kumquats, peels only
2 habanero chiles, cut in half, stem and seeds removed, cut into ¼-inch strips
1 cup kosher salt (Minh suggests Jacobsen's salt)

METHOD

– Place kumquat peels and chiles on a rack set onto a half-sheet baking pan for air circulation. Place the pan in a warm oven overnight.

– Grind the kumquat peels, chiles, and salt in a mortar and pestle or pulse in a food processor to combine.

– Pour salt mixture onto a parchment-lined baking pan; place on your kitchen counter to dry overnight.

– Store salt in a tightly sealed jar. It will keep indefinitely.

FOOD SOURCES: Negi at Thao Family, T & D, and Yasutomi farms, which have booths at the Hollywood Farmers' Market. Makrut limes and leaves are at most Asian markets, including 168 Market, H Mart, and Marukai Market. If you don't have access to geranium leaves, any edible floral leaf or floral substitute, such as citrus, marigolds, jasmine, and basil flowers, will work. I rely on neighborhood foraging, with permission.

ROASTED PEPPERS

Preheat oven to 450°.

INGREDIENTS

6 to 8 red, orange, and yellow sweet peppers
3 to 4 tablespoons olive oil to coat the peppers
Good-size pinch kosher salt

METHOD

- Slice off the top of each pepper or twist off stem and remove the pith and seeds by pulling these out through the top of the pepper.

- Cut each pepper into 6 to 8 pieces lengthwise. Combine with olive oil and salt in a large bowl so that peppers are lightly coated (I mix all by hand until combined).

- Spread on parchment-covered half-sheet pan. Place pan on middle rack of oven and roast for 20 to 30 minutes. The peppers' skin should be wrinkled and brown in some places, and the peppers should have shrunk as their juices released.

- Remove from oven. Tip peppers into a bowl and cover with plastic wrap.

- When they have cooled, remove the skin by pulling it off carefully. Store peppers in a covered jar. These keep up to a week in the refrigerator.

TRY THIS: These peppers make a delicious addition to a sandwich (goat cheese with Roasted Peppers, for example, or on top of an open-face melted-cheese sandwich); to a salad with goat cheese and arugula or other spicy greens; or to pasta with butter and parmesan. They also make an excellent accompaniment to roasted chicken or pork.

You may use the same method for roasting poblano or other chiles with heat. These are great with quesadillas or other Mexican-influenced foods. Wear rubber gloves when peeling hot peppers, as the capsaicin oil in these peppers can burn your skin, eyes, and anywhere you touch.

FOOD SOURCES: I often rely on Armenian or Mexican markets. The peppers are gorgeous, fresh, and of a variety rarely seen. Don't be afraid to ask a friendly store clerk or shopper about heat level and use. I have learned a lot from these folk. Armen Market, Super King Markets, and Vallarta Supermarkets are all great places for peppers and for produce in general.

TAKA'S PICKLES

As you can probably tell, I like pickles. One of my favorites is the Japanese pickle called Tsukemono. This recipe has history, coming from my friend Taka Suzuki's mother. These are delicious as a light salad on their own or served as a contrast to a rich protein, such as salmon or black cod.

Makes 6 pints

INGREDIENTS

3 pounds Persian cucumbers, cut into spears
6 tablespoons salt
10 cups water, divided
6 cloves garlic, crushed
6 generous slices fresh peeled ginger
6 whole dried red peppers (Tianjin red chiles are a good choice)
1 cup white vinegar
8 tablespoons sugar

METHOD

– Sterilize 6 large-mouth pint Mason jars (I run them through a cycle in my dishwasher).

– Place cucumber spears into a large heat-proof bowl.

– Place salt and 2 cups water in a 3-quart saucepan; bring to a boil over high heat.

– Pour the hot, salted water over the cucumbers and let sit, uncovered, for 1 hour.

– Drain cucumbers.

– Into each sterilized jar add 1 clove garlic, 1 slice ginger, 1 dried pepper, and as many cucumber spears as will fit.

– Combine vinegar, sugar, and 8 cups water in a large bowl; mix until sugar is dissolved.

– Pour pickling mixture into each jar and affix lid.

– Refrigerate immediately. Store pickles for up to 1 month.

TRY THIS: Add 5 to 6 thin slices peeled ginger or 3 to 4 sprigs fresh dill per jar.

FOOD SOURCES: Armenian and Asian markets such as 168 Market, Armen Market, H Mart, and Marukai Market have good Persian cucumbers for a reasonable price.

MARGIE'S SWEET AND SOUR CUCUMBERS

My stepmother Margie's Scandinavian heritage is revealed in this recipe.

Makes 1 quart

INGREDIENTS

1 pound Persian cucumbers (These are the smallish, slender cucumbers with thin skin.
   Do not use the short pickling cucumbers, as they are too bitter.)
Kosher salt
1 cup white or rice vinegar, more if needed
½ to 1 cup sugar

METHOD

– Slice the cucumbers into very thin rounds, about ¼ inch thick.

– Place a layer of rounds on a large plate.

– Cover rounds with a thin layer of salt. (I pour salt into a bowl and spoon salt over
   the cucumbers.)

– Continue layering with cucumbers and salt until all cucumbers are layered.

– Let cucumbers sit, allowing the liquid to drain out of the cucumbers.

– After about 2 hours or more, rinse the cucumbers thoroughly under cold water,
   then squeeze small handfuls of cucumbers until most liquid is squeezed out.
   The cucumbers will be limp.

– Place cucumbers in a 1-quart glass storage container or jar and add vinegar and about
   half as much sugar—enough liquid to cover the cucumber slices.

– Taste to assure the right combination of saltiness and sweetness.

– Allow the cucumbers to rest in the liquid for at least 3 hours to overnight.

TRY THIS: Add a few slices of fresh ginger or a few sprigs of fresh dill, along with
vinegar and sugar; for a bit of heat, add 1 tablespoon chile flakes with vinegar and sugar.
Pickles may be served as a small salad. They provide a piquant taste for open-face
sandwiches, especially with bay shrimp and mayonnaise, and add flavor to Fried Rice
(see page 134). Because these cucumbers are pickled, they should keep in your
refrigerator at least 3 weeks.

"My Korean ancestry hasn't only influenced how I perceive the world, but more so
my palette. I love pickles! From taste to preparation to experience, Elisa explains
each step."
ESTHER KANG, *novice cook, self-described millennial, recipe tester*

Margie's Sweet and Sour Cucumbers
with Twenty-One Hour Boule (see page 96).

EDIBLE PLATES

Some of the simplest and most delicious meals start with what I call the edible plate. These are variations on starch—admittedly my favorite food group—that holds food, whether a small scoop of dip, a layer of cheese with sautéed vegetables, or a custard cheese filling. Although this list is brief, you will find these plates to be the basis for invaluable variations to your cooking. For example, one of my end-of-the-week habits is "refrigerator foraging," in which I repurpose bits and pieces of cheeses and sautéed vegetables into a delicious shortbread-crusted quiche. You will be more than proud of this transformation from homely end-of-life scraps to exquisite meal—and you will be reducing food waste, too.

CRESPELLES
Based on Marcella Hazan's *Essentials of Italian Cooking*.

Both crespelles and crêpes are incredibly versatile as wrappers for both savory and sweet fillings. They are my go-to rescue for "bits and pieces" of leftover cheese, meat, stew, or fruit. Crespelles are lighter than crêpes, as there is no butter in the batter. They can be used in place of pasta for filled dishes such as cannelloni or in Ricotta Crespelles with Sage Butter Sauce (see page 82). If using them for dessert, add a bit of sugar or maple syrup to the batter.

Makes 16 to 18 very thin pancakes

INGREDIENTS
1½ cups whole milk
1 cup all-purpose flour
2 large eggs (3 if smaller)
¼ teaspoon salt
1½ to 2 tablespoons salted butter

METHOD
– Put milk in a medium bowl and add flour gradually, sifting it through a sieve if possible, while you mix steadily with a fork or whisk to avoid lumps.

– When you have added all the flour, beat the mixture until it is evenly blended.

– Add the eggs, one at a time, beating them in rapidly with a fork or whisk.

– When eggs have been incorporated into the batter, add salt, stirring to distribute.

– Lightly smear the bottom of a 5- to 7-inch nonstick skillet with a small amount of butter—no more than ½ teaspoon.

– Place pan over medium low heat.

– Give the batter a good stir and pour 2 tablespoons into the pan.

– Tilt and rotate the pan to distribute the batter evenly.

– As soon as the batter sets and becomes firm, slip a spatula underneath the crespelle and flip it over to cook the other side.

– Add the remaining butter bit by bit as needed, and continue making the crespelles.

FRENCH CRÊPES

I have rarely found a cook who does not love the versatility of this slender pancake. This recipe is based on a favorite from *The Fannie Farmer Cookbook*.

Makes about 15 crêpes, depending on thickness

INGREDIENTS
2 eggs
1 cup milk
½ teaspoon salt
1 cup unbleached all-purpose flour
2 tablespoons salted butter, melted, plus more for cooking the crêpes

METHOD
– Beat eggs well, then beat in the milk, salt, flour, and melted butter.

– Cover mixture and let stand for at least 30 minutes.

– Heat a 5- to 7-inch nonstick skillet over medium-high heat until moderately hot, then spread a film of butter onto the pan using a brush or folded paper towel. Ladle 3 to 4 tablespoons batter into the pan.

– Quickly tilt the pan so the batter spreads evenly in the thinnest possible layer.

– Cook for a few minutes, until the bottom is lightly browned and the edges lift easily from the pan.

– Turn the crêpe with a spatula or by catching an edge with your fingers and flipping it over. Continue cooking for a minute or so, until crêpe is a very light golden color. (The first crêpe is usually a "throwaway" snack, as it is not perfect.)

– Crêpes may be made ahead, then cooled, stacked, wrapped in plastic wrap, and refrigerated. They will stay fresh for several days.

TRY THIS:
TURMERIC CHILI CRÊPES
The bright yellow color is a beautiful surprise. Add 2 teaspoons chili powder, 2 teaspoons turmeric, 2 teaspoons honey, and 1 teaspoon salt to the basic crêpe batter. Serve with lightly salted ricotta. These also work well as a substitute for naan or roti for curry or highly spiced stews.

BUCKWHEAT CRÊPES
Follow the basic crêpe recipe above with the following changes: Combine ¾ cup buckwheat flour with ½ cup all-purpose flour; increase milk to 1½ cups and eggs to 3.

DESSERT CRÊPES
Add the following to the basic crêpe batter: 5 teaspoons demerara or brown sugar, freshly ground nutmeg (4 to 5 passes over a microplane), 2 teaspoons ground cinnamon, and 1 teaspoon vanilla extract. Substitute unsalted butter. Serve with jam and whipped cream.

FOOD SOURCES: Excellent flour may be purchased at Grist and Toll.

CROUTONS

Simple Croutons, Pita Chips, and Crostini are great for salads, especially Caesar salad, and as a topping for soup.

Makes about 2 cups

INGREDIENTS

1½ teaspoons extra-virgin olive oil
Leftover (day-old or more) country white bread, ciabatta, or baguette, cut into ¼- to 1-inch cubes (I usually use the last of the bread once it begins to get stale—about a quarter of a loaf).
Generous pinch kosher salt

METHOD

– In a medium skillet, heat olive oil over low heat.

– Add cubed bread and sprinkle with salt.

– Toast very slowly on all sides.

– Remove from heat, cool, and store in a resealable plastic bag until ready to use.

PITA CHIPS

Better than store-bought, these are lighter and actually low-calorie—yay!

Makes about 4 cups

Preheat oven to 300°.

INGREDIENTS

6 fresh white-flour pitas
½ cup extra-virgin olive oil
Kosher salt

METHOD

– Slice the bottom of each pita bread; open the bread into 2 circles by carefully separating the top and bottom.

– Cut each circle into quarters to make triangles.

– Brush with olive oil, and salt lightly.

– Bake on a parchment-lined half-sheet pan for about 20 minutes, until crisp.

– Store in a large, tightly covered jar or resealable bag.

TRY THIS: For even thinner and crunchier crackers that have the texture of potato chips without the calories, use whole-wheat lavash flatbread in place of pita bread. Cut the lavash into generous 3-inch squares. Follow the last three steps for Pita Chips, but reduce the baking time to 8 to 10 minutes.

FOOD SOURCES: Berolina Bakery & Pastry Shop, Lincoln, or Seed Bakery for baguette; Armen Market for pita bread and lavash.

CROSTINI

The basis for a number of appetizers.

Makes 40 to 60 crostini, depending on how you slice

Preheat oven to 325°.

INGREDIENTS

1 rustic baguette
⅓ cup extra-virgin olive oil
Kosher salt

METHOD

- Slice baguette thinly, straight or diagonally, and place on parchment-lined half-sheet pan.

- Brush olive oil lightly onto each slice of bread and sprinkle sparingly with kosher salt.

- Bake until crispy and light brown, about 20 minutes.

- Remove from the oven, let cool on a baking rack, and store in a resealable plastic bag. Keeps for at least 1 week.

TRY THIS: Slice crostini straight across for small rounds or on the diagonal for larger, oval pieces, depending on how you plan to use them.

Spread with pesto and grated parmesan cheese; broil 2 to 5 minutes—take care not to burn. Other toppings could include olive tapenade, fresh goat cheese with roasted peppers, herbed ricotta chese, or thinly sliced parmesan with olive oil. They can also be served as a very fine neutral cracker for a cheese platter. Thanks to Minh's Pantry Essentials, I have some delicious new spreads for crostini. Try adding Minh's Negi Oil or Minh's Makrut Compound Butter (see page 48) as a first layer on your crostini—wow!

FOOD SOURCES: Great crostini start with great bread: in this case, a baguette. A joyful way to taste-test baguettes is by visiting your local bakeries or cheese specialty shops. Here are a few of my favorite places for delicious bread: Europane, Seed, Lincoln, and Little Flower bakeries. Cheese stores usually carry good-tasting baguettes as well: try The Cheese Cave, Milkfarm, or Say Cheese. Cookbook always has great freshly baked bread.

SHIRLEY MOORE'S PILAF

Armenian food varies depending on place of origin, including the Middle East, Russia, and Armenia itself, but pilaf is a standard throughout. Shirley (or Shami) Moore was a good friend of my father's, Sy, and stepmother, Margie. Her family was Armenian, and she was an excellent, traditional cook. After marrying Pat Moore, she continued to cook Armenian dishes, greatly simplified, as she and Pat became the proud parents of three active boys. This recipe became a family favorite because of its deliciousness and ease.

Makes 4 servings (½ cup each)

INGREDIENTS

1 to 2 tablespoons unsalted butter
Small handful (about 20 pieces) vermicelli pasta (can use spaghetti in a pinch)
1 cup long-grain rice
1 teaspoon kosher salt, if using homemade chicken broth
2 cups chicken broth, store-bought or homemade (see How to Make Chicken Broth the Easy Way, page 35)
Few gratings nutmeg (optional)

METHOD

– Melt butter in large saucepan until foamy.

– Break vermicelli in 1- to 2-inch pieces and add to the melted butter, cooking over low heat until it darkens a bit. Add rice and continue cooking until the rice is slightly golden. This will smell delicious.

– Add salt if using homemade chicken broth.

– While waiting for the rice to turn color, heat the chicken broth in another saucepan, or microwave in a heat-proof container, until almost boiling.

– Add the hot chicken broth to the rice mixture, stir to combine, reduce the heat to simmering, and cook, covered, for 20 to 30 minutes, until rice has absorbed all the liquid.

– Uncover the pan, let sit a minute or two, and fluff the rice.

TRY THIS: Add ½ cup blanched, toasted almonds and 1 tablespoon minced flat-leaf parsley warmed in about 1 tablespoon butter as a topping for the pilaf.

Serve with roasted chicken, tri-tip, or any simple meat. Pilaf is great as a favorite breakfast treat known in the Callow household as Cheesy Rice. Spoon some pilaf in a heat-proof dish; grate whatever cheese you have over it, and heat in the oven or microwave.

SLO-MO POLENTA

According to Bill Buford's account in *Heat*—my favorite food memoir—polenta has been cooked all wrong in this country: too little water, too short a cooking time, and too much stirring. A number of trusted sources concur, and after trying their methods, I can confirm that what he says is true. Cooking begins with a much higher ratio of water to grains, low heat, and infrequent rather than constant stirring. Pick a day when you are planning to nest to try this delicious dish.

Serves 6 as an appetizer, 4 as a main dish

INGREDIENTS

4 cups water

2 teaspoons kosher salt, or more

1 cup coarse polenta

2 tablespoons unsalted butter

1 cup grated parmesan or pecorino cheese to taste, additional grated cheese as a topping

METHOD

– In a 4-quart saucepan over medium heat, bring 4 cups water to a simmer. Add salt.

– Slowly add polenta in a steady stream, whisking as you add.

– Whisk for a couple minutes to avoid lumps. Increase heat and cook until polenta comes to a low boil; cook 1 to 2 minutes. Reduce heat, keeping at a low simmer.

– With a wooden spoon or heat-proof spatula, give the polenta a good stir every now and then. When it absorbs all the water, add more water, ¼ cup at a time. Continue to stir occasionally.

– After 1 to 2 hours, the polenta will be done. You will know because the granules will have become creamy and soft.

– Remove polenta from heat, add butter and grated cheese, and stir well. Add more cheese as a topping or serve cheese on the side. Polenta keeps refrigerated, covered, for up to 5 days.

– If you plan to cut the polenta into squares, let it cook a little longer, until it pulls away from the sides of the pan. Or you can pour it into a heat-proof casserole dish and let it cool before cutting it into squares.

TRY THIS: Polenta is one of the most versatile of dishes, with a consistency similar to grits. I have used chicken broth in place of water for a richer tasting dish, reducing the salt to 1 teaspoon and tasting before adding more. I have also combined 1 cup milk with 5 cups water to start. Purists may be horrified, but I find all versions delicious.

Serve polenta as is with chopped herbs, more butter, and grated parmesan cheese. You can fry squares in olive oil, then top them with pesto, marinara sauce, or fried mushrooms and more parmesan cheese. Polenta is a delicious breakfast cereal topped with maple syrup and cream.

FOOD SOURCES: Most supermarkets sell polenta, but Italian specialty markets offer more variety. Stone-ground polenta has a more rustic, uneven texture. You can find polenta at Claro's Italian Markets, Eagle Rock Italian Bakery and Deli, and Roma Italian Deli and Market. For freshly ground polenta, try Grist and Toll.

SHORTBREAD CRUST and How to Fill It

This is my go-to crust for all savory tarts. It is delicious and easy, and serves as a perfect base to transform end-of-the-week bits of cheeses, vegetables, or meats into an elegant dish. I increase this recipe by half when I am making a savory tart for a crowd, and have used this crust for all sizes of pans and numbers of eaters—including just me. Keep an eye on the proportion of flour to butter, salt, and sugar, and you will be fine. The dough can rest until you have time to make the tart.

Makes a 10-inch crust, about 8 medium slices

INGREDIENTS
2 cups unbleached all-purpose flour
Pinch kosher salt
¾ cup (1½ sticks) unsalted butter, chilled, cut into ½-inch cubes, plus more for pan
1 tablespoon sugar

METHOD
– Combine all ingredients in a medium bowl; mix, using a pastry blender or your fingers, until the dough is the texture of rough sand.

– Dribble in cold water, if needed, until mixture barely holds together.

– Take two generous pieces of plastic wrap, crossing one length over the other. Carefully pour dough mixture onto the center of the plastic wrap.

– Pull up the plastic, consolidating the dough as you do so. Create a disc about 1½ inches thick and 6 inches across. Refrigerate at least 3 hours or overnight.

– When you are ready to prepare the tart, preheat oven to 425°.

– Generously butter a 10-inch pie or tart pan (I prefer those with removable bottoms).

– Push small pieces of chilled dough into the bottom of the pan and up the sides. Smooth with your hands, as this is much too short a crust to roll out. Make sure to create a relatively thin layer of crust, about ⅛ to ¼ inch. I use a rounded coffee cup or canning jar to push the crust into the sides more evenly.

– Blind bake crust for 10 minutes, remove from oven, and cool for a few minutes before filling. (To blind bake, prick the crust with a fork; then cover with foil and fill with dried beans to keep crust from shrinking.) I sometimes blind bake the dough in the morning and fill and finish baking in the evening if time is short.

– Store any remaining dough wrapped in plastic in the refrigerator. It will last a few days more for your next foraging adventure.

TRY THIS: Start all savory fillings with a custard: Beat 2 to 3 eggs with ¾ cup cream, half and half, or whole milk. One or 2 thinly sliced caramelized onions may be added to savory tarts, such as those that follow. To caramelize onions, slice the onions thinly. Add 1 tablespoon salted butter to a medium frying pan. Cook over medium-high heat, stirring constantly, until onions are translucent. Reduce heat to low and continue cooking slowly, stirring once in a while until onions are golden to very light brown in color and very soft. They should taste sweet and mellow.

Slice 2 beefsteak tomatoes (or quarter 4 smaller, very ripe tomatoes), add 5 or 6 leaves of thinly sliced basil, and heat in a frying pan over low heat for less than a minute. Arrange heated vegetables over blind-baked shortbread crust. Add ½ cup grated parmesan and spoon in 6 ounces soft, fresh goat cheese. Finish by pouring custard carefully around the filling.

Arrange 5 or 6 spears cooked asparagus on crust; add 6 ounces soft goat cheese in spoonfuls and ½ cup grated parmesan. Pour custard around filling.

Combine 1 cup cooked corn, 8 ounces grated jack cheese or queso Oaxaca, and 2 tablespoons crema or Crème Fraîche (see page 38); place in crust and pour custard around filling.

In a small frying pan over low heat, sauté 1 cup thinly sliced cooked zucchini and a few nutmeg gratings in 1 tablespoon butter. Add to crust; top with 2 to 3 thin slices of ham and 8 ounces grated gruyère cheese; pour custard around filling.

In a small frying pan over low heat, cook 1 thinly sliced onion and 2 to 3 sage leaves in 2 tablespoons unsalted butter until onion is caramelized. Remove sage leaves and add mixture to crust, along with thinly sliced baked winter squash and 6 ounces goat cheese; pour custard over filling.

For a lighter tart, use whole milk in the custard. I add an extra egg to ensure that the custard sets, and I often grate some nutmeg into the custard mixture for flavor. You can use caramelized sliced leeks in place of onions. You can also double the vegetable filling, using dark greens such as swiss chard or kale, lightly sautéed in butter until wilted, to fill the crust. Use only about ¼ cup parmesan or other dry cheese.

For savory custard-filled tarts, bake at 350° for 35 to 40 minutes, or until custard is set. The middle should barely jiggle.

To make a sweet tart, add 2 tablespoons sugar and about ¼ cup ground, lightly toasted almonds to the dough.

For a simple dessert, spread a layer of good-quality jam on the crust. Add enough pitted and sliced apricots, peaches, or plums to generously cover the surface of the crust. Sprinkle mixture with 1 tablespoon demerara or granulated sugar and distribute 1 tablespoon diced unsalted butter across the top.

Bake sweet tarts at 350° for 20 to 25 minutes, until bubbly.

FOOD SOURCES: Try different flours in your crust for added flavor. Grist and Toll, Cookbook, and Armen Market are great places to buy high-quality and, in, some cases, freshly ground flour. For the fillings, make sure to visit your local farmers' market for the freshest of all fruits and vegetables.

Sumi Chang rolling out dough.

HOW TO MAKE A PIE CRUST

My husband, Eric, is the pie baker in our home, having learned as a young boy from his mom, Charlotte, and his Aunt Beanie, pie-baking masters. He has reached and exceeded their proficiency. His go-to pie crust recipe can be found in Rose Levy Beranbaum's *The Pie and Pastry Bible;* Eric adds an additional ¼ to ½ teaspoon salt.

The most important thing about good pie crust is to make sure that all ingredients are chilled to begin with, and kept cold throughout the process. For butter or any other form of shortening, that means refrigerating or even freezing the ingredients prior to use. Butter or shortening should be evenly cubed: Slice butter into ¼-inch slabs, cut these into 3 to 4 sticks, then cube the sticks by cutting them perpendicularly from the end. Return cubed butter to the refrigerator or freezer until use.

The second most important thing is not to use too much water. The length of time you spend working the shortening into the flour will affect the way in which the flour takes up water. I suggest cutting in the initial portion of shortening for at least 2 to 3 minutes. Do not use more water than the recipe suggests; rather, be patient and let the dough rest to allow the liquid to distribute. Work the dough into as cohesive a ball as you can, wrap it in plastic, and let it rest for at least 1 hour in the refrigerator.

When blending, use a sustained pressure with the pastry cutter to work the butter or shortening into the flour. The butter or shortening should be introduced in two successive portions. This allows the fat and the flour to be integrated without overworking the dough. After resting, it will be easier to roll out. Handle the dough as little as possible.

When ready to roll out the dough, spread a layer of flour on a pastry cloth, and coat the dough ball with a healthy dusting of flour. When rolling, the motion always starts from the center out, as it rolls the flour in a consistent direction and stretches it evenly.

Once you have rolled out your dough, use the pan as a form to cut the dough about 1 inch beyond the radius of the pan. This will also expose gaps in the edge of the dough. You can cut off excess dough scraps and paste them onto bare spots with water to smooth out the edges.

To transfer the dough disc, place your forearm under the pastry cloth and lift up the dough and the pastry cloth (which supports the dough). Match the edge of the dough with the edge of the pan so that 1 inch extends beyond it, then roll the dough into the pan.

If you don't have a modern convection oven, which ensures even heat, cover the edges of the pan with a pastry guard or foil to avoid burning the crust.

NOTE: Shortening refers to butter; vegetable shortening, such as Crisco; or lard. These can be used singly or in combination.

Jam, Marmalade, and More

"It's all jammed up here. Blackberry. The seeds are in my teeth, the ichor, all over. I'm drenched. These are the days, my friends. The days wherein one realizes what kind of creature one really is. And I, jammies, I find myself: often a creature who's got blackberry jam all over his mitts. Mitts jammed in face."
CHRISTOPHER ROUNTREE, *breakfast guest, leader of wild Up modern music collective, friend*

JAM AS MUSE HAIKU
Still slow with sleep I
pry back the sticky lid whose
taste pulled me from bed
ELLEN REID, *breakfast guest, composer, friend*

Sunday morning at the Hollywood Farmers' Market, one of many sources for great fruit—an essential ingredient for jam-making.

ALYSE JACOBSON'S STONE-FRUIT JAM—Peach, Apricot, or Plum

This is Alyse's recipe for any type of stone-fruit jam, and it is truly the best. It can be doubled easily. Do not triple, however, as jam can scorch when too much volume prevents it from cooking evenly. Apricot is most people's favorite—and one of the easiest because you don't have to peel the apricots.

I learned the trick of adding 2 to 3 tablespoons of Grand Marnier from my jam-making friend in Germany. Julia swears by the liqueur's ability to hold flavor and prevent spoiling. I like how it tastes—adding depth without overwhelming.

A note on the jam-making fad—I am all for it! Take time to look at the artisan jams sold at farmers' markets and specialty-food stores, as these jam-makers are unbowed by tradition and offer many interesting flavor pairings, such as rose water, pepper, and geraniums.

Makes 6 to 7 cups

EQUIPMENT

6 to 7 8-ounce (half-pint) canning jars
Copper jam pan (If you don't have this specialized equipment, it is best to use a low, wide pan that holds at least 8 quarts. Wider pans help the liquid to evaporate—a requirement for jam to thicken and gel. Do not use copper for citrus or other acidic fruits and vegetables unless sugar is added.)
Immersion blender
Jam funnel
Jar lifter
Lid holder
Ladle
Large, deep stockpot for sealing and sterilizing filled and sealed jars (the "hot water bath" process)

INGREDIENTS

9 cups fruit, cut into ½-inch chunks
6 cups sugar
Juice of 1 lemon
1 to 2 tablespoons Grand Marnier (optional)

METHOD

– Begin by sterilizing the jars. This is important! I run jars and their outer rings in the dishwasher and keep them hot. Sterilize inner lids in boiling water for a few minutes, using the lid holder.

– If making peach jam, you will need to prepare the fruit with a bit more care. Peel peaches using a sharp vegetable peeler with a serrated edge or submerge them in boiling water for 10 to 15 seconds, then remove and peel. Cut fruit in half, remove pit, and cut away the red "fringe" around the pit. Chop each peach half into sections and cut those into 3 additional pieces; they should be medium bite-size pieces. If making apricot or plum jam, you need only to remove the pit. There is no "fringe" around plum or apricot pits to worry about. Plum peel adds gorgeous color and tartness to the jam.

– Add prepared fruit to jam pan. Mix in sugar and lemon juice.

– Let mixture sit for 30 minutes, until juices draw out; this will help prevent scorching. Stir over low heat until sugar melts. Raise heat and bring mixture to gentle boil; cook until mixture is pourable, like a thick syrup. Continue cooking, checking temperature with a candy or jam thermometer.

– If making apricot or plum jam, add Grand Marnier just before jam reaches gel point.

– Cook until gel point is reached, about 45 minutes total (see chart below for gel point).

– Use an immersion blender to chop up most of the fruit to a "rustic" purée—smooth with some chunkiness. Take care to leave the blender below the surface of the jam mixture, or you will most surely burn yourself with hot flying jam.

– Fill stockpot ¾ full with water and bring to a low boil.

– Place jam funnel on lip of sterilized jar and ladle jam mixture into jar. Repeat for each jar. Leave about ¼ inch between jam and top of jar.

– Wipe jar rims thoroughly with a clean, damp paper towel (I dip the paper towel into the boiling water prepared for the sterilizing bath). Close the jars, but not too tightly. Place jars in pot and cover with 2 to 3 inches of water. Cover pot and sterilize jars at a low boil for 10 to 12 minutes.

– Remove jars with jar lifter and let cool on a wire rack. You should hear a pinging sound as the jars seal.

– When cool, remove outer rings and check each jar to be sure the lids are tightly sealed. Dry the outer rings to prevent rust and screw them back on the next day, when jam is cool.

Jam gel-point temperature is based on altitude, as the chart below illustrates:

Sea Level to 1500 feet	218°
1500 to 3000 feet	214°
3000 to 4000 feet	212°
4000 to 5000 feet	211°
5000 to 6000 feet	209°
6000 to 7000 feet	207°

NOTE: If the inner lid does not seal properly after the water bath, simply try again by making sure the jar lid and outer ring are aligned correctly. You will need new inner lids, but can reuse the outer rings. Resterilize the jars in the dishwasher, and repeat processing as directed. Take care to pay attention to gel-point temperature. It is better to err on the side of undercooked, as the jam tends to firm up after sitting overnight. If the jam remains too loose, boil the jam for a few more minutes to thicken, and finish as directed.

FOOD SOURCES: For seasonal fruit, check the list of producers represented at farmers' markets and go to their websites to see what they have available. Pasqual from Rancho Padre Farms (at the Pasadena Certified Farmers' Market) sells wonderful stone fruits. Try "foraging" from friends with apricot or plum trees in exchange for a jar of jam. Homegrown is my best source for the harder-to-find, heirloom varieties of fruit.

STRAWBERRY JAM

Kevin West says it most convincingly in his beautiful and informative cookbook, *Saving the Season: A Cook's Guide to Canning, Pickling, and Preserving:* Buy in season. I wait for the smaller seascape and Chandler varieties of strawberries, but let your taste buds be your guide. After purchasing, begin canning as soon as possible; these little red delights do not last.

Refer to Alyse Jacobson's Stone-Fruit Jam recipe for equipment, gel point, and canning instructions (see pages 70 and 71).

Makes 4 pints or 8 to 9 cups
(Do not attempt to double this recipe, as cooking increases the volume.)

INGREDIENTS

4 pounds ripe strawberries, cleaned and dried
2 pounds sugar
2 tablespoons lemon juice
1 tablespoon good-quality balsamic vinegar
10 to 15 grinds black pepper

METHOD

– Cut berries in half and then into 2 to 3 slices for each half.

– Combine fruit with sugar and lemon juice in a large 6-quart pan or copper jam pan.

– Let sit until strawberries release a bit of juice, about 30 minutes.

– Mash with a potato masher and then heat until boiling.

– Cook until mixture reaches gel point, stirring frequently to avoid burning the jam. The jam will increase in volume and look very, very foamy. Do not worry; it will calm down and lose most of its foaminess. You will also see the jam changing from an opaque, lighter red color to a beautiful, deep-red jewel tone. This is a good time to add the balsamic vinegar and the pepper, and to begin checking the temperature for the gel point.

– When mixture reaches gel point, remove pan from heat and place on a rack to cool for a few minutes. Skim off foam; I use a rubber bowl scraper.

– Can jam as directed (see previous two pages).

FOOD SOURCES: Strawberries during their peak in late May and June are a whole different fruit from those sour, hard, hollow berries grown out of season. Farmers' markets are your best bet. The stands along Highway 126, north of Los Angeles, are another good source. If you are planning a trip to Santa Barbara or Ojai, consider taking this route home, as it is also a window into California's farm history (see page 237).

CITRUS MARMALADE

Great for gifts and oh, so good! This marmalade lasts about one year stored in a cool pantry.

See Alyse Jacobson's Stone-Fruit Jam recipe for equipment needed and gel point (see pages 70 and 71).

Makes 3 to 4 pints or 6 to 8 cups

INGREDIENTS

5 large seedless oranges (navel or blood), sliced
4 lemons
8 cups water
7 cups sugar
3 tablespoons Grand Marnier

METHOD

– Cut oranges and lemons in half crosswise, then into very thin half-moon slices. Discard seeds.

– Place sliced fruit into a stainless steel pot. Add 8 cups water and bring mixture to a boil, stirring often. Remove from heat and stir in sugar until dissolved. Cover and allow to stand overnight at room temperature.

– The next day, pour mixture into a copper jam pan or large sauté pan. (It is safe to use a copper pan at this point because the sugar will prevent the citrus from reacting to the copper.)

– Return mixture to a boil and reduce heat to medium at a very low boil. Simmer, uncovered, for 2 hours. Stir once in a while, every 15 minutes or so. During this time, liquid evaporates continuously. Toward the end, the marmalade will thicken and become more jewel-like in color: golden orange or saffron, depending on the fruits used. At this point, check the temperature; stop cooking when it reaches the gel point for your area. Another way to check doneness is to spoon a bit of marmalade onto a plate that has been placed in the freezer for a few minutes. The marmalade should be thick but not hard, and not too runny. You should be able to draw a clean line through the marmalade with your finger.

– Follow the canning directions for Alyse Jacobson's Stone-Fruit Jam, as noted above.

TRY THIS: Marmalade can be made with most varieties of citrus fruits. Two favorites are Rangpur lime and Meyer lemon marmalade. These are more tart than naval or blood orange marmalades, reflecting the character of the fruit.

FOOD SOURCES: Lily and Steve's Porch Market, Sprouts Farmers Market, and farmers' markets. You can forage close to home by placing a notice in your neighborhood blog inquiring about excess citrus fruit. This is how I found the rare and wonderful Rangpur lime tree growing in neighbors Elizabeth and Paul Barber's backyard. I always provide a jar of marmalade in exchange for fruit.

MULBERRY JAM

Lily Knight and I are on-again off-again jam-making partners, an arrangement that works beautifully. She supplies the fruit; I supply the other ingredients and most of the jars. It is so much more fun doing something that requires care and time with a good friend.

See Alyse Jacobson's Stone-Fruit Jam recipe for equipment needed and gel point (see pages 70 and 71).

Makes 2 to 3 pints or 4 to 6 cups

INGREDIENTS
9 cups Pakistani mulberries
8 cups sugar
Juice of 1 medium lemon
1 apple with core and peel, cut into quarters
Zest of 1 orange
1 teaspoon vanilla extract
Dash Grand Marnier

METHOD
– Strip the mulberries from their stems using your hand or a rose-thorn stripper. Discard the stems. (Wear gloves, unless you like magenta.)

– Place mulberries, sugar, lemon juice, apple pieces, and orange zest in a jam pan or in a low, wide-bottom 8-quart pan. Stir and let sit for 15 minutes.

– Heat over medium-high heat, stirring frequently to avoid scorching.

– Continue cooking until temperature reaches 2 degrees below gel point.

– Add vanilla and Grand Marnier and continue cooking until reaching gel-point temperature. (This takes a long time, be patient.) Stir frequently.

– Remove apple core. Finish jam as noted above.

NOTE: Apples are a good source of natural pectin and add thickening power to this jam.

FOOD SOURCE: Pakistani mulberries at Lily and Steve's Porch Market and farmers' markets in season, late April through June.

SPICED PEACHES

Summertime means foraging farther afield to the remaining farming areas of Southern and Central California—or heading to your local farmers' market.

Makes about 5 quarts canned peaches

INGREDIENTS

3½ teaspoons whole allspice
3½ teaspoons whole cloves
14 cinnamon sticks
10 pounds ripe peaches (heirloom are truly better)
Thin or Medium Simple Syrup, depending on preference for sweetness (see page 44)

METHOD

– Sterilize 5 quart-size jars and their rings by running them through a quick dishwasher cycle. Hand wash the inner seals with soapy water and rinse.

– Place spices into jars: ½ teaspoon each allspice and cloves, and 2 cinnamon sticks per jar.

– Fill a medium bowl with ice water. Bring a large pot of water to a boil. Blanch peaches by dipping each into boiling water for up to 60 seconds. Remove with a slotted spoon and place into ice water to stop the cooking.

– Immediately slice each peach in half. Slip off skin, loosened by the hot water bath.

– Remove peach pit and any fragments of the pit. Place peaches into jars, cut-side down, fitting peaches as tightly as you can; they will shrink a bit over time.

– Cover with hot syrup up to about ½ inch from the top. This is called "head space," and allows a vacuum to be created in order to seal the jars. Make sure the mouth of the jar is clean. Close with seal and ring. Place in deep pot and cover with water at least 2 inches above the jars. Boil for 30 minutes. (If you live in an elevation higher than 1,000 feet, locate canning instructions for adjusted time requirement.)

– Remove jars. Place on rack to dry and cool. Check seal by removing the outer rings. The seals should be on tight. If not, reprocess or refrigerate and consume within 1 week.

– Store jars in a dark, cool place. Peaches will keep for at least 1 year.

TART PIE CHERRIES

Once you understand how to can peaches, tart pie cherries are easy. For tart pie cherries, try Armenian markets in June.

INGREDIENTS

10 to 12 pounds tart cherries
Thin Simple Syrup (see page 44)

METHOD

– Follow canning instructions for Spiced Peaches with the following changes: Wash and dry cherries. Remove pits with a cherry pitter. (You will want at least two of these and a friend.) Omit the spices. Fill, process, and store as you would for Spiced Peaches. Use cherries in pie, or in Tart Cherry Soup (see page 115).

CANDIED ORANGE PEEL
Adapted from *Canal House Cooking, Volume No. 3*.

In my experience, most candied orange peel is sticky, too sweet, and somewhat weird tasting. This recipe is the opposite—sublime. You will find yourself mincing small pieces of candied peel and adding them to yogurt, ice cream, hot cereal, buttered toast— anything that would benefit from the refreshing bite of citrus.

Makes about 1 cup

INGREDIENTS
3 thick-skinned oranges (navels work well, as do blood oranges)
2½ cups sugar, divided
2 cups water
1 vanilla bean split and seeds scraped out, or 1 teaspoon vanilla extract
2 to 3 sprigs fresh rosemary

METHOD
– With a very sharp paring knife, slice rind away from oranges as widely as possible. You will want fat slices. Carefully remove all the pith so that you have only the rind left.

– Put peels into a heavy, medium saucepan and cover with cold water. Bring to a boil, then drain. Repeat with fresh water, boil, and drain. Leave peels in the pan.

– Add 2 cups sugar and 2 cups water, vanilla bean seeds or extract, and rosemary to the pan. Bring mixture to a boil over high heat.

– Reduce heat and simmer, uncovered, for 1 hour, until liquid becomes a thick syrup.

– Using tongs, remove peels one at a time and let dry on a cooling rack until sticky.

– Dredge pieces in remaining ½ cup sugar. Dry on a rack overnight. Store in an airtight container. Orange peels stay fresh up to 3 weeks.

NOTE: To remove vanilla seeds from bean, carefully cut bean in half lengthwise. With the tip of a knife, remove the seeds. They are a bit sticky and will clump together.

FOOD SOURCES: Oranges are available year-round, but better in season at Cookbook, Sprouts Farmers Market, and farmers' markets.

Breakfast and Brunch

Roe Sie of The King's Roost in Silver Lake, milling wheat berries into flour.

RICOTTA CRESPELLES WITH SAGE BUTTER SAUCE

Rich, delicious, and a great brunch dish.

Serves up to 6, depending on appetite (2 to 3 filled crespelles each)

INGREDIENTS

18 Crespelles (see page 56)
¼ cup unsalted butter, melted
6 or more fresh sage leaves
1 pound good-quality whole-milk ricotta
½ to ¾ cup freshly grated parmesan cheese
A few gratings nutmeg
½ teaspoon salt, more if needed
Freshly ground pepper

METHOD

– Prepare the Crespelles. You can do this the night before, but make sure they are at room temperature when you start to assemble, or they will not separate easily from one another.

– Heat oven to 350°.

– Melt butter in a small pan over medium heat. Add sage leaves; be careful not to break them.

– Brush a small amount of sage butter in a 3-quart rectangular or oval baking dish. Let remaining butter continue to heat until foamy. Carefully remove cooked sage leaves to a small plate.

– In a small bowl, add most of melted sage butter, ricotta, parmesan, nutmeg, salt, and pepper. Combine thoroughly. Taste and add more salt if needed.

– Add a hefty tablespoon of ricotta mixture to each crespelle, spreading mixture into a cigar shape.

– Roll each crespelle around the ricotta "cigars" and place in a large gratin dish, seam-side down.

– Pour remaining sage butter over rolled crespelles. Grate a bit more parmesan over crespelles.

– Place warmed sage leaves on top for decoration. Heat crespelles in oven for about 20 minutes, until cheese is bubbly. Serve and swoon.

FOOD SOURCES: For the ricotta, Eagle Rock Italian Bakery and Deli, Claro's Italian Market, Roma Italian Deli and Grocery.

SUMI'S FRITTATA

For all of us whose day improved immeasurably when eating breakfast at Europane, here is one of Sumi Chang's delicious and easy-to-make standards. "A frittata is an Italian dish with eggs and vegetables, traditionally cooked on top of the stove and then baked to finish. I use a baking pan, as I bake it in the oven." (See Sumi's profile on page 195.)

Serves 6

Preheat oven to 300°.

INGREDIENTS

3 Italian kale leaves
2 tablespoons olive oil
1 medium shallot, finely chopped
½ medium clove garlic, finely sliced
1 bunch swiss chard leaves, ribs removed, washed, liquid squeezed out, and chopped
10 large eggs
½ cup cream
½ teaspoon dried oregano or 1 teaspoon fresh oregano, minced
½ teaspoon fresh Italian parsley, minced
2 sprigs fresh tarragon, or any other delicate fresh herb, finely chopped
¼ teaspoon dried sage or 1 to 2 fresh sage leaves, finely chopped
Pinch red chile flakes
¼ cup freshly grated parmesan cheese (optional)
1 teaspoon kosher salt
½ teaspoon black pepper
½ cup ricotta cheese

METHOD

– Grease an 8-inch round or square baking pan with nonstick spray or butter. Add parchment cut to size on the bottom of pan to help frittata release easily.

– Place kale leaves in a hot skillet until toasted, a couple of minutes. Set aside.

– In the same skillet, reduce heat to medium-low and add oil and shallots. Then add the garlic and continue cooking until shallots and garlic are translucent.

– Add the chard, cooking until soft. Set aside. When cooled, use a towel to squeeze out liquid from the mixture. You should have 1 cup of chard, shallots, and garlic combined.

– In a bowl, whisk eggs, cream, herbs, chile flakes, parmesan, salt, and pepper.

– Spread vegetables evenly in greased pan. Then add egg mixture.

– Add ricotta cheese in dollops to the top of the mixture. Place kale leaves on top.

– Bake for 1 hour. Check for doneness by sticking a toothpick into the middle of the frittata. When done, it will come out clean. If not, bake up to 20 minutes more.

– Let cool. Use a small spatula or butter knife to release the sides, turn frittata out onto a plate, and then turn over again onto a serving plate, kale-leaf side up.

TRY THIS: Substitute other vegetables such as spinach, zucchini, corn, sweet peppers, or a combination of these. Try fried, crumbled sausage or diced bacon. Whatever variation you use, go for 1 cup total of the vegetable or vegetable/meat combination.

CRANBERRY, ALMOND, AND CINNAMON GRANOLA

Lower in calories than most granolas, but still delicious.

Makes about 6 cups

Preheat oven to 350°.

INGREDIENTS

4 cups old-fashioned rolled oats
1½ cups sweetened shredded coconut (or unsweetened coconut, if you prefer)
2 cups slivered almonds, lightly toasted
1½ cups dried cranberries
½ cup vegetable oil
¼ cup honey or maple syrup
2 teaspoons ground cinnamon
½ teaspoon salt

METHOD

– Toss oats, coconut, almonds, and cranberries together in a large bowl.

– Combine vegetable oil and honey or maple syrup and pour over the oat mixture.
  Add cinnamon and salt.

– Stir with a large, flat spoon or your hands until all of the oats and nuts are coated
  with the liquids. Pour onto a parchment-lined half-sheet pan.

– Bake, turning over once halfway through with a spatula, until mixture is a nice,
  even golden brown, about 25 to 30 minutes total.

– Cool completely. Store in an airtight container for up to 1 month.

NOTE: Nuts have different toasting times—and the smaller the pieces, the shorter the
toasting time. For the slivered almonds, scatter over a parchment-lined half-sheet pan.
Bake at 350° for 5 to 8 minutes.

FOOD SOURCES: Aladdin Nuthouse, Sprouts Farmers Market, farmers' markets.

"This recipe brokered my newfound love for DIY granola. I even tried making the second batch with almond butter. When the mind grabs onto something, it runs with it."
ESTHER KANG, *novice cook, self-described millennial, recipe tester*

DOUG'S PANCAKES

Despite being very healthy, these pancakes are very good. The batter lasts for days in the refrigerator and is a great workday dish.

Serves 6

INGREDIENTS

2 cups whole-wheat flour

1 cup oatmeal (do not use instant)

¼ teaspoon salt

2 tablespoons sugar

1 to 2 teaspoons baking soda

3 eggs, separated (you will need 1 yolk and 3 egg whites)

2 tablespoons oil

3 cups buttermilk

2 to 3 tablespoons butter

Syrup (maple or fruit) or jam

METHOD

– Combine all dry ingredients.

– Add egg yolk and oil to buttermilk.

– Add this mixture to dry ingredients.

– Whip up egg whites and fold into the batter.

– Heat a nonstick skillet. Add half the butter and melt until foamy. Add a half ladle (about ¼ cup) of batter to the heated butter until the pan is full—4 to 5 separate pancakes. Cook about 1 minute on each side, until browned and a little crispy.

– Serve with syrup or jam.

FOOD SOURCES: Cookbook for buttermilk, eggs, and flour. Grist and Toll, Cookbook, or Armen Market for flour. The King's Roost sells whole grains and various countertop mills, if you're up for an investment in milling your own flour.

EASY AND HEALTHY APPLE CRUMBLE—for Weekday Mornings

Enjoy! Tastier than oatmeal, but just as healthy.

Serves 5 to 6

Preheat oven to 350°.

INGREDIENTS

4 apples good for cooking—gala or pink lady work well
3 tablespoons unsalted butter
1 cup rolled oats
¼ cup sugar (granulated, light brown, or demerara)
½ teaspoon salt
Pinch cinnamon
1 teaspoon vanilla extract

METHOD

– Peel, core, and slice apples thinly.

– Heat half of the butter in a frying pan over medium-high heat, stirring occasionally; add apple slices and cook until softened, about 5 minutes.

– Remove apple slices and place in an overlapping pattern in an oval baking dish.

– Add remaining butter to the same pan and melt over low heat.

– Add oats, sugar, salt, cinnamon, and vanilla; stir until oats are coated and a bit toasty.

– Spread oat mixture over sliced apples.

– Bake for 35 to 40 minutes.

– Serve with whipped cream, if desired.

"The apple crumble was so good, I had to force myself to put some away for the next morning's coffee."
BETSY CLANCY, *novice cook, recipe tester*

BLUEBERRY PUDDING CAKE

Great for brunch or dessert, this can be made ahead, cooled completely, then wrapped well in foil and kept at room temperature for at least one day. Or you can prepare everything up until baking and store in the refrigerator covered with plastic wrap. Bake when your guests arrive, and serve hot.

Serves 4 to 6

Preheat oven to 375°.

INGREDIENTS

⅓ cup plus ½ cup sugar

1 tablespoon fresh lemon juice

1 teaspoon cornstarch

¼ cup water

10 ounces (2 cups) fresh, good-quality blueberries

1 cup all-purpose flour

1¾ teaspoons baking powder

1 teaspoon salt

1 large egg

½ cup whole milk

½ cup (1 stick) unsalted butter, melted and cooled slightly

1 teaspoon vanilla extract

METHOD

– Place oven rack in middle position.

– Butter a 9-inch-square baking pan or ovenproof oval pan of equivalent size.

– Stir together ⅓ cup sugar, lemon juice, cornstarch, and ¼ cup water in a small saucepan. Stir in blueberries. Bring to a simmer and cook for 3 minutes, stirring occasionally. Remove from heat.

– In a medium bowl, whisk together flour, baking powder, salt, and remaining ½ cup sugar.

– In a large bowl, whisk together egg, milk, melted butter, and vanilla. Add the flour mixture, whisking until just combined.

– Spoon batter into baking pan or ovenproof oval casserole, then pour blueberry mixture evenly over batter (berries will sink).

– Bake until a knife inserted into center of the cake comes out clean, 25 to 30 minutes.

– Cool in pan, on a rack, 5 minutes.

OVER-THE-TOP FRENCH TOAST

For this french toast, even the best challah (egg bread) won't do. Buy brioche bread or panettone at a good bakery—the richness of butter-filled bread really makes a difference.

4 to 5 servings, depending on appetite (2 slices per person)

INGREDIENTS

1 medium loaf brioche or panettone
5 to 6 eggs
Zest of 1 orange
¼ cup fresh orange juice
1 tablespoon Cointreau or Grand Marnier
3 tablespoons unsalted butter, more if needed

METHOD

– Cut bread into 8 to 10 slices, about 1/2-inch thick.

– In a flat pan, mix eggs, zest, orange juice, and Cointreau or Grand Marnier. Soak each bread slice in egg mixture, coating both sides.

– In a large, flat frying pan, heat butter over medium heat until foamy.

– Add soaked bread, one layer at a time. Cook until crispy, about 3 minutes, then turn over and crisp the other side.

– Place french toast on a heated platter in a warm oven—about 200°—until all toast slices are done.

– Serve with raspberries, maple syrup, or jam (apricot is great).

FOOD SOURCES: Panettone is a seasonal bread, most readily available during Christmastime; loaf-shaped brioche works just as well. Eagle Rock Italian Bakery and Deli, Europane Bakery, Proof Bakery, Roma Italian Deli and Grocery, Seed Bakery—or for the slight taste of rosemary, Julienne.

SAVORY DOUBLE PECAN SCONES

Great for guests, as you can easily double this recipe, and the baked scones freeze quite well.

Makes 16 scones

Preheat oven to 350°.

INGREDIENTS

1¼ cups pecans
2¼ cups all-purpose flour
2 teaspoons baking powder
½ teaspoon baking soda
½ teaspoon salt
½ cup salted butter, cold
4 ounces (1 cup) gruyère cheese, shredded
½ teaspoon dried thyme, crushed, or 1½ teaspoons finely chopped fresh thyme
1 egg, lightly beaten
1 cup buttermilk
1 tablespoon honey
1 tablespoon Dijon mustard

METHOD

– Place pecans on a baking sheet and bake for 5 to 7 minutes, or until toasted. Coarsely chop 1 cup of the pecans; finely grind remaining ¼ cup pecans. I use a coffee grinder. Set aside.

– Increase oven temperature to 375°.

– In large bowl, combine pecans, flour, baking powder, baking soda, and salt.

– Using a pastry blender or your fingertips, cut or pinch in butter until mixture resembles coarse meal.

– Stir in gruyère, 1 cup coarsely chopped pecans, and thyme.

– In a small bowl, combine egg, buttermilk, honey, and mustard; add to flour mixture. Using a fork, stir until just moistened.

– Turn dough out onto a lightly floured surface. (The flour makes the dough less sticky.)

– Knead dough by folding it over and gently pressing for 10 to 12 strokes, or until nearly smooth.

– Divide in half (if doubling, divide into quarters). Pat or lightly roll each half into a ¾-inch-thick circle, about 6 inches in diameter.

– Cut each circle into 8 triangles. Place triangles on parchment-lined half-sheet baking pan.

– Bake 18 to 20 minutes, or until golden.

– Transfer to cooling rack. Serve warm.

FOOD SOURCES: Aladdin Nuthouse for pecans; Sprouts Farmers Market and Cookbook for pecans and dairy products.

TWENTY-ONE-HOUR BOULE

Also known as No-Knead Bread, this recipe is adapted from *Pure Vegan,* by Joseph Shuldiner, and based in turn on a recipe by Jim Lahey of Sullivan Street Bakery in New York. There are so many versions of it because it is so incredibly easy and delicious.

Makes one 2-pound loaf

INGREDIENTS

500 grams flour
¼ teaspoon active dry yeast (I buy mine at Smart & Final—the big box of yeast)
35 grams vital wheat gluten, optional (can be purchased online)
2 teaspoons salt
¼ cup olives, walnuts, pecans, or seeds (optional)
415 grams or more distilled water

METHOD

– In a large bowl, combine flour, yeast, vital wheat gluten, and salt; mix well. Mix in optional savory ingredients.

– Add distilled water and stir until well blended. Dough should be wet and fairly sticky.

– Cover bowl with plastic wrap and let rest in a warm spot for 18 hours. After this first rise, dough will be at least double in volume and small bubbles will have formed on the surface.

– Using a flour-dusted dough scraper or spatula, scrape dough onto a clean, lightly floured work surface. Coat your hands with flour and gently pat dough with your palms to create a thick disk. Tuck under the circumference of the disk to create a round ball. Turn the disk over, round-side down. With both hands, gently reach under the dough and stretch the tucks in a bit more. Re-flour dough. Don't fret over this step; each time you make this loaf you'll become more familiar with the bread and how to shape it.

– Flour a banneton (wooden proofing-bowl), then place the ball of dough in the banneton, rough side up.

– Dust dough with more flour and cover with a tea towel. Let dough rise for 2 hours, until it doesn't readily spring back when poked with a finger.

– About 30 minutes before the end of this second rise, put a lidded 6- to 8-quart Dutch oven or heavy ovenproof pot into the oven, and preheat oven to 475°.

– When the oven has preheated and the Dutch oven is hot, about 30 minutes, carefully remove pot from the oven.

– Flip the banneton and hit it forcefully into the hot Dutch oven to release dough from the banneton.

– Remove the banneton while taking care to avoid the sides of the hot Dutch oven. Cover the pot, return it to the oven, and bake for 30 minutes.

– Uncover the Dutch oven and bake for 15 minutes or a bit more, until boule is browned and sounds hollow when tapped.

– Remove from oven and immediately transfer boule to a rack to cool. (Do not attempt to cut the boule until it's cool, or you will get mush.)

NOTE: The ingredients need to be weighed rather than measured by volume to ensure accuracy. Use a cooking scale. However, the amount of water varies depending on what is known as the absorption rate of flour. You will want a fairly gloppy dough for first rise.

Many bread bakers are turning to "wild yeast," made with flour, water, and the healthy bacteria around us and in the flour. This is the starter that adds the tang to sourdough bread. Try this when you are feeling more confident. So delicious!

FOOD SOURCES: Cookbook or Grist and Toll. For bulk orders, Los Angeles Bread Bakers via The King's Roost.

"I consider myself a somewhat accomplished cook, but a baker I am not. Elisa encouraged me to take a stab at her Twenty-One-Hour Boule. I kept telling myself, 'This is not going to work, this is not going to work.' Miraculously, it does, and the results are so sublime that I might even buy myself a baker's hat. This is now my go-to bread."
BILL ANAWALT, *experienced cook, recipe tester*

SLOW SCRAMBLED EGGS WITH PROSCIUTTO

The trick to these eggs is to be patient and cook them over very low heat. The result is amazingly creamy, soft eggs.

2 to 4 servings, depending on appetite

INGREDIENTS

4 slices rustic bread, sliced about 1/2 inch thick
1 tablespoon unsalted butter or olive oil, for bread
1 clove garlic, peeled and cut in half
6 eggs, room temperature
2 tablespoons butter, divided, for eggs
¼ teaspoon kosher or gray sea salt
Freshly ground pepper
4 thin slices prosciutto

METHOD

– Brush bread slices on both sides with butter or olive oil.

– Toast bread in a large skillet over medium-high heat until browned on both sides, about 6 minutes.

– Rub each slice with cut garlic and set aside.

– Whisk eggs together with 1 tablespoon butter cut into pieces.

– Melt remaining 1 tablespoon butter in a 9-inch nonstick skillet over very low heat. Add eggs and cook, still over very low heat, stirring occasionally, until they begin to set on the bottom, about 2 minutes.

– Continue to cook, stirring almost constantly, until eggs become creamy, with a texture resembling small-curd cottage cheese. Continue cooking and stirring until eggs begin to thicken and become less glossy but are not quite done, 8 to 15 minutes.

– Remove eggs from heat and stir for about 1 minute to finish cooking. They should be very creamy, with very small curds.

– Divide eggs onto toasted bread and spread over each slice. Add a pinch of salt and a grinding of black pepper to each slice. Top each serving with a slice of prosciutto.

TRY THIS: Substitute Minh's Negi Oil (see page 48) for butter when scrambling the eggs. Or substitute for the prosciutto a few small slices of smoked dried chorizo, chopped finely, and 2 finely chopped scallions. Begin by adding chorizo and scallions to the frying pan over low heat until heated through and the fat has flavored the pan. Then add egg and butter mixture. Finish with a generous grating of parmesan cheese.

FOOD SOURCES: For bread, Berolina Bakery and Pastry Shop, Europane Bakery, Seed Bakery—or your own Twenty-One Hour Boule (see page 96). For eggs, Cookbook, Culture Club 101, farmers' markets.

SUNDAY QUESADILLAS

When I asked Michael Martinez—head of L.A. Compost and one of L.A.'s emerging leaders in the healthy food/environmental movement—about his favorite sustainable meals, he mentioned Sunday Quesadillas. His family repurposes "bits and pieces"—aka leftovers—from the week and uses tortillas as a base for whatever looks good. For my Sunday Quesadillas, I found some triple cream cheese, beet greens, Crème Fraîche (a staple in my refrigerator, see page 38), and green onions. They were delicious! I use freshly made and mixed masa, as the few extra minutes to roll, press, and heat a tortilla is minimal effort for the reward of fresh taste and texture.

Serves 1 (this recipe may be increased by adding tortillas and multiplying additional ingredients accordingly)

INGREDIENTS
¼ to ⅓ cup prepared masa for tortillas
Scant teaspoon vegetable oil
Beet greens (from 1 to 2 beets)
1 green onion, ½ inch of green end removed
¼ cup or less mild cheese, such as manchego or havarti
1 tablespoon Crème Fraîche (see page 38)

METHOD
- Form masa into a ball and place between 2 plastic sheets in a tortilla press, or roll into a flat round with a rolling pin. The size of the ball will determine the size of your tortilla. I usually make the ball a little larger than a golf ball.

- In a large nonstick pan, heat vegetable oil over medium heat. Add tortilla and cook until slightly toasted; then turn over and repeat toasting. Remove from pan.

- In the same pan, heat beet greens and green onion until slightly wilted. Remove from pan.

- Return tortilla to pan. Add a few gratings or small chunks of cheese to tortilla; heat over medium-low until cheese is melted. Remove to plate. Add beet greens and green onion, and drizzle with Crème Fraîche. Serve hot.

TRY THIS: The ingredients used here are just one of many topping combinations that can be found through refrigerator foraging. Try bits of stew meat and roasted vegetables. A favorite of mine is melted cheese topped with pan-heated corn and various leafy greens.

FOOD SOURCES: Prepared masa can be purchased at Mexican supermarkets such as Super A Foods or Vallarta Supermarkets for convenience. Even better are smaller specialty stores, such as La Mayordomia Market and La Princesita Carnicera y Tortilleria. I usually buy only a pound or so, which causes some raised eyebrows, as this is a relatively small amount. Be sure to ask for the masa for tortillas versus tamales.

BAKED EGGS TIMES THREE

These are easy, but they do require a bit of care.

4 to 8 servings (1 to 2 baked eggs per person)

Preheat oven to 325°.

INGREDIENTS

Scant amount butter or Minh's Negi Oil (see page 48)
1 cup whole milk or half-and-half
4 to 8 eggs, room temperature
2 to 3 ounces grated cheese (your choice)
2 to 3 thin slices deli ham

METHOD

– Butter or oil 4 to 8 ramekins.

– In a small pan over low heat, bring milk or half and half to a simmer.

– Crack 1 egg into each ramekin. Add warmed milk or half-and-half, cheese, and ham.

– Place ramekins in a 3-quart heat-proof rectangular baking dish or equivalent. Place pan into oven and carefully pour hot water two-thirds up the sides of the ramekins (this will maintain moisture in oven while eggs are cooking).

– Bake for about 10 minutes. Watch carefully. As soon as egg whites become opaque and yolks begin to get firm, remove eggs from oven—you want soft yolks.

TRY THIS:

CHORIZO WITH CRÈME FRAÎCHE

– Fry a bit of finely chopped dried chorizo and about 1/2 cup chopped arugula.

– Heat 1 cup whole milk with 2 tablespoons Crème Fraîche (see page 38), a few gratings of nutmeg, and a pinch of salt.

– Place chorizo and arugula into each ramekin and grate a bit of parmesan cheese on top. Crack in 1 egg. Add about ¼ cup milk mixture, salt, and pepper. Bake as above. When done, top each ramekin with more grated parmesan.

MUSHROOM, GRUYÈRE, AND GOAT CHEESE

– Fry about ½ pound small, thinly sliced mushrooms in a bit of butter until mushrooms are dry and almost crisp, about 10 minutes. Add salt and pepper to taste.

– Heat 1 cup whole milk or half-and-half with 1 tablespoon fresh goat cheese; blend with a whisk or fork. Add a few gratings of fresh nutmeg.

– Add mushrooms and 1 tablespoon finely chopped parsley to each ramekin. Crack in 1 egg. Pour ¼ cup warm milk mixture into each ramekin. Top with a few generous gratings of gruyère. Bake as above.

– Top each ramekin with a large pinch of parsley.

Mario Rodriguez in his Highland Park garden, holding his mother's *molcajete*.

PROFILE: MARIO RODRIGUEZ

Some of us are born with a golden spoon in our mouths—most everything we taste is a potential treasure to be collected into our food palate memory. For the imaginative and confident cook, each taste experience enriches our palate awareness, inspiring an ongoing process of replication, adaptation, and the creation of ever-new recipes and tastes. In the case of my friend Mario Rodriguez, a discussion about food memory and influences lasted well into the night. His memories encompass both generation and geography: the Rodriguez, Contreras, and Lujan families that represent farm, town, and city life in Mexico and the Southwest, as well as the rich diversity of Los Angeles's food culture.

From the farm, there is Abuelita Maria, his paternal grandmother, who lived in San Acacia, New Mexico, near Socorro, where she raised sheep and searched for piñon nuts. She made candies and syrups in a small copper pan handed down to Mario, who plans to reproduce her delicious quince syrup. His Uncle Toño, one of Maria's sons, hunted rabbit and *pichon* to be transformed into stews flavored by pipián moles. His Tía Victoria also lived out in the country in Mira Valles, Nayarit state, in Mexico. This was where Mario first learned to milk a cow—he likens the taste to a warm, rich milkshake. Everything was fresh: corn tortillas, produce, meat.

Town dweller Tía Rita, a resident of Chihuahua, Juarez, Mexico, is described as a flavor-profile queen who filled delicious freshly baked *bolillos* with bologna, mayo, avocado, and cheese. In contrast to this salty goodness, there was always Coca Cola—an appetizing combination for young Mario.

And in Los Angeles, Mario's father Chuy's idea of fun was to bracket errands with eating by searching for the perfect *morcilla*, fried hushpuppies, and *lumpia*. Nothing was off-limits to his dad, including truck food, of which he was an early patron. As a supervising social worker for Los Angeles County, Mario travels for work, which allows him to follow his dad's habit of lunchtime food explorations. Mario's mother, Lupe, remains his most consistent teacher, handing down her expertise in making pozole, chiles rellenos, and *tortitas de camarón con nopales y chile colorado*.

Mario's wife Monica's stepmother, Mavi, from Escuinapa, Sinaloa, just south of Mazatlán, is a maker of the intensely flavored *ceviche de camarón*, a sauce made of dried shrimps spiced with habanero chiles. Monica's brother Luis is a master baker, recently relocated to Eureka, California, to expose these far-northerners to great bread. Monica herself is no slouch, traveling near and far for authentic ingredients for the family's frequent and beautifully executed communal feasts. Monica's longtime friend Patricia provides another link to Mario's growing food family. Patricia is married to David Féau, a well-known L.A. chef originally from France. David led Mario to the Truffle Brothers, extraordinary purveyors of many things Italian, especially truffles. Mario and David redefine tamales in their annual tamale-making fest; David's latest favorite is filled with foie gras.

Mario and Monica's daughter, Paloma, is well on her way to attaining the rarefied status of fearless gourmet. When I last saw her, the nine-year-old quizzed me on my method of whipping cream, a very good sign.

MARIO RODRIGUEZ'S FOOD INFLUENCES

Dad (Chuy)
Chuy, the omnivore. No food off-limits!

Abuelita Maria
Paternal grandmother; made candies and syrups.

Mavi
Wife Monica's stepmother; a maker of ceviche de camarón.

Tía Victoria
Paternal aunt; fresh milk, tortillas, and meat.

Luis
Wife Monica's brother; master baker.

David Féau
Los Angeles chef and friend; participant in Mario's annual tamale-making fest.

Mom (Lupe)
The constant in Mario's food education; pozole, tortitas de camarón con nopales.

Abuelita Brijida
Maternal grandmother; her metate was used for hand grinding corn tortillas.

Uncle Toño
Paternal uncle; hunted rabbit and *pichon* to make stew.

Tía Rita
Maternal aunt; filled bolillos with bologna, mayo, avocado, and cheese.

Tía Eva
Maternal aunt; owned small café serving sopes and gorditas for factory workers.

Monica
Mario's wife, a great cook herself; co-maker of the family's celebratory paella.

Truffle Brothers
Friends of Mario; Los Angeles-based source of great truffles and cheese.

Soups Many Ways, All Healthy

MARIO'S POZOLE

Mario Rodriguez's inheritance from his mother and grandmother includes learning to make pozole. Mario has tweaked his version of this dish to coax out layers of flavor and brightness.

Serves 8 to 10

INGREDIENTS for Meat and Stock

5 pounds pork-neck bones (espinazo)
1 large or 2 small brown onions, peeled and cut into quarters
8 large cloves garlic, peeled and left whole
1 large or 2 small bay leaves
2 pounds pig feet, cut in quarters (or substitute 2 pounds bone-in chicken thighs)

METHOD

– Place pork-neck bones in large Dutch oven or sturdy pot with onion, garlic, and bay leaves.

– Cover with water plus a couple of inches and cook over high heat until boiling.

– Reduce to a low boil and continue to cook for at least 20 minutes. Remove the scum.

– Turn heat down to a simmer, cover, and cook for 1 hour. Remove scum again.

– Add pig feet or chicken thighs and continue to simmer for 1 additional hour. The broth should be rich and flavorful after 2 hours; if watery, cook for another hour.

INGREDIENTS for Chile Sauce (to be completed after meat and stock have been prepared)

2 dried guajillo chiles
2 dried New Mexico chiles
1 dried chipotle chile, for smokiness
2 cups meat stock

METHOD

– While meat is simmering, toast chiles on a hot skillet or comal until flexible, about 5 minutes. Split open chiles and remove seeds. In a medium saucepan over high heat, cover chiles in water (a cup or so). Boil for 5 to 10 minutes; chiles will become soft. Strain chiles and blend with 2 cups meat stock in a food processor or blender (sauce will be watery).

INGREDIENTS for Combining Meat, Stock, and Sauce

2 to 3 pounds nixtamal (so much better than canned hominy, which can be used in a pinch)
3 to 5 tablespoons salt

METHOD

– In a 3-quart saucepan, cover nixtamal with water. Bring to a boil and cook 3 to 4 minutes.

– Drain, reserving 1 to 2 cups of the flavorful liquid.

– Remove meat from neck bones. Shred meat; return to broth. Remove bay leaves.

- Remove pig feet or chicken thighs; set aside to serve alongside pozole.

- Ladle nixtamal into stock. Add chile sauce and reserved nixtamal cooking liquid.

- Add 3 to 5 tablespoons salt, tasting as you go.

- Simmer 1 additional hour, for a total of at least 3 hours.

INGREDIENTS for Serving

10 radishes, thinly sliced
Large bunch cilantro, chopped
10 or more key limes, cut in half
El Paraiso brand Home Style Tostadas (fried tortillas)
Small bowl dried Mexican oregano
Shredded cabbage
Chopped avocado

METHOD

- Ladle pozole into serving-size bowls, adding a pig foot or chicken piece for each serving. Place accompaniments on a platter so that each person may choose desired type and amount. Squeeze limes into the pozole for a tart, crisp counterbalance to the rich broth.

FOOD SOURCES: El Mercado de Los Angeles, La Princesita Carnicera y Tortilleria, Super A Foods, Vallarta Supermarkets for pork-neck bones, pig feet, chiles, nixtamal, and limes. Don't be afraid to ask the clerks for help if you feel unsure about ingredients; it works!

The entrance to El Mercado de Los Angeles, in Boyle Heights.

SUMMER CORN CHOWDER

Serves 4

INGREDIENTS

4 ears fresh corn, shucked

1 to 2 tablespoons unsalted butter

½ medium onion, cut into 1/2-inch dice

½ medium russet potato, peeled and cut into ½-inch dice

1 large pasilla chile, seeded and cut into ½-inch dice (omit if you do not want heat)

About 1 teaspoon kosher salt, divided

Freshly ground black pepper to taste

1¼ cups chicken broth

3 cups whole milk

2 small scallions, finely chopped

Pinch cayenne pepper

Crème Fraîche (see page 38), optional

METHOD

– Remove corn from cobs; set kernels and cobs aside.

– In a medium saucepan over medium heat, melt butter, then add corn kernels. Cook until color changes to a darker yellow. Remove corn from pan and set aside.

– Add a bit more butter, then add onions, potato, chile, ½ teaspoon salt, and pepper.

– Allow mixture to caramelize slightly over low heat, about 5 minutes.

– Add chicken broth to saucepan and half of the corn; cook until potatoes are fork tender, about 10 minutes.

– While vegetables and chicken broth are cooking, heat milk and the corn cobs gently in another saucepan. (This will impart even more corn flavor.) Remove cobs after about 10 minutes and turn heat off.

– Pour cooked vegetables, broth, and half of the heated milk into a blender. Purée for about 1 minute.

– Return mixture to the saucepan and add remaining corn kernels, scallions, and remaining milk.

– Cook another 10 minutes on a low simmer. Do not let soup boil, or it will curdle and separate. Add more salt and pepper to taste.

– Serve with a sprinkling of cayenne pepper and 1 teaspoon Crème Fraîche, if desired.

NOTE: To remove corn kernels safely, cut the pointed end off of the corn. Set cob on a cutting board cut-end-side down, and carefully cut the kernels off the cob. If the soup curdles, cool and then reblend for a minute.

FOOD SOURCES: Sprouts Farmers Market, farmers' markets.

RICH MUSHROOM SOUP

The variety of mushrooms really adds to the flavor of the soup. For example, dried porcini and shiitakes have more concentrated flavor than fresh ones.

Serves 6

INGREDIENTS

2 ounces dried porcini mushrooms
2 tablespoons butter
3 sprigs fresh thyme
1 onion, diced
1 large shallot or 3 small, diced
1 teaspoon kosher salt
10 or so grindings fresh pepper
8 ounces fresh cremini mushrooms, coarsely chopped
6 cups purchased or homemade chicken stock (see pages 34 and 35)
½ cup dry white wine
2 egg yolks
½ cup heavy cream

METHOD

- Soak dried mushrooms in ½ cup hot water to hydrate, about 15 minutes.

- In a large, heavy pot (Le Creuset is great) over medium heat, heat butter until foamy. Add thyme, onions, shallots, salt, and pepper. Continue to cook over medium heat until onions and shallots are soft and somewhat caramelized (browned to allow for rich flavor), about 15 to 20 minutes. Remove thyme.

- Add cremini mushrooms to onion mixture and continue to cook over medium heat.

- Drain hydrated porcini mushrooms through a fine sieve, reserving liquid (the sieve strains out any debris from the mushrooms). Add strained liquid to chicken stock. Remove porcini mushrooms from the sieve and add to onion mixture.

- When mushrooms have browned, add wine. Allow wine to reduce and flavor the vegetables.

- Pour stock mixture into the vegetables. Heat until lightly simmering; reduce heat to low and continue cooking for 30 minutes.

- In the meantime, mix egg yolks with cream in a small bowl. When vegetable mixture is hot, add about 1 cup of the broth to egg and cream mixture to prevent yolk from curdling. Set mixture aside.

- When soup has cooked for about 15 minutes, use a slotted spoon to strain the solids (mushrooms, shallots, and onions) to a blender, adding a cup of the broth to help liquefy mixture. Blend for 1 minute.

- Return vegetable mixture to broth and stir. Soup should be thick, like smooth gravy.

- Add egg and cream mixture. Stir and warm for another 10 minutes.

- Add salt and pepper to taste.

FOOD SOURCES: For mushrooms, 168 Market, Cookbook, H Mart, Marukai Market, Surfas Culinary District, farmers' markets.

MADZOONEH SHORBA (YOGURT SOUP)

This was a beloved soup among customers at the Aghoian family's restaurant (see profile page 139). It is a very gentle-tasting, yet tart soup with a complex flavor, despite its simple ingredients. As with many family recipes, there is room for your own preferences. The more yogurt you add, the tarter the soup and the thinner its consistency. I found the soup's flavor deepened after a couple of days.

Serves 6 to 8

INGREDIENTS

1 cup pearled wheat or pearled barley
4 cups water
2 to 3 cups plain whole-milk yogurt
1 egg or 1 egg white
Salt to taste, about 1 tablespoon
A few pinches finely minced dried mint

METHOD

– Place pearled wheat or barley in a large bowl; add warm water to cover.

– Let wheat soak overnight. (If using barley, you will need to soak it longer, at least 24 hours.)

– The next day, boil 4 cups water in a 6-quart pot with a lid.

– Drain wheat or barley and add it to the boiling water.

– Reduce heat to simmer, cover pot, and continue cooking 45 minutes to 1 hour. Watch that the soup does not overflow; very low heat will prevent this. The pearled wheat should completely open up, releasing gluten, which thickens the soup. You should have about 2 quarts of cooked wheat.

– In a small bowl, mix together yogurt and egg, then add to wheat. Continue cooking on low heat for 10 minutes. Add salt.

– To serve, add a generous pinch of dried mint to each portion.

NOTE: Mary Aghoian dries mint from her garden. She removes the leaves to dry on a half-sheet pan in the shade of a backyard tree for a couple of weeks, then crumbles the leaves and stores them in a jar labeled Ganesha Mint, named after her street. Dried mint has a more robust flavor, so do not substitute fresh.

FOOD SOURCES: Pearled wheat, pearled barley, and dried mint are staples at most Armenian grocers, such as Armen Market. Cookbook, Culture Club 101, and Garni Meat Market carry excellent whole-milk yogurt without additives. Or you can make your own (see page 40).

ARPY'S MUJETDEREH (LENTIL SOUP)

This simple but exacting recipe comes from my friend Arpy Gendahl's grandmother and was later modified by Arpy and her mother. It's a delicious dish that provides a perfect and healthy backdrop to other Armenian delights, such as feta and string cheese, pita bread "scoops," and fried cauliflower.

Serves 8

INGREDIENTS for Fried Shallots

½ cup unbleached flour
Pinch sea salt
Pinch cayenne pepper
4 shallots, sliced thinly in rings
¾ cup vegetable oil

METHOD

– Mix flour, salt, and cayenne pepper. Lightly coat shallots with flour mixture.

– In a small saucepan, heat oil until a test piece of prepared shallot fries quickly, between 325° and 375°. Fry shallots in small batches until golden brown. Drain on a thick layer of paper towels and set aside.

INGREDIENTS for Soup

2 cups small, gray-green lentils (often called French puy)
½ cup long-grain rice
6 cups water
1 large onion, minced, divided
½ cup olive or vegetable oil
About 2 teaspoons sea salt to taste
About ½ teaspoon cayenne pepper to taste

METHOD

– Remove debris from lentils; wash lentils and then rice in a fine-mesh sieve.

– In a large saucepan over high heat, bring 6 cups water, lentils, and rice to a boil. Reduce heat to medium-low and continue cooking, partially covered, until nearly all of the water is absorbed, about 45 minutes. Do not stir or rush.

– Halfway through, add ¾ cup raw minced onion.

– When water is almost completely absorbed and the soup is the consistency of oatmeal, heat oil in medium frying pan; deep-fry remaining minced onion until pieces become small, light brown bits, called *sokhratz.* Pour oil and fried onion bits into lentil mixture. Season with salt and cayenne pepper to taste.

– At this point, the soup is about done. There will be a small amount of water remaining. With a large spoon, mash lentils against the side of the pan and stir. Serve hot, garnished with fried shallot rings. Dish will be creamy and rich.

NOTE: *Sokh* is onion and *ratz* is short for *ayratz,* which means burnt. This is my short lesson in how food is a delicious entry into culture and language.

TART CHERRY SOUP with Lemon Thyme and Vanilla

If you can find good-quality canned pie cherries, you can make this delicious, light, and unusual dessert. I include a recipe for Tart Pie Cherries, which is quite easy to make if you are able to find this elusive fruit (see page 77).

Serves 6

INGREDIENTS

24 ounces canned pie cherries (three 8-ounce cans)
Thin Simple Syrup (see page 44)
5 sprigs lemon thyme
2 makrut lime leaves
½ Meyer lemon, cut into thin slices
1 vanilla bean, split open and seeds scraped out, or 2 teaspoons vanilla extract
6 scoops strawberry sorbet or vanilla ice cream or 6 tablespoons mascarpone cheese

METHOD

– Drain cherries; reserve liquid in a 2-quart measuring container. Add Thin Simple Syrup to equal 4½ cups of liquid. Place cherries in a separate bowl.

– Combine syrup, thyme, lime leaves, lemon slices, and vanilla in a medium saucepan. Cook slowly, covered, for 30 minutes. Remove lime leaves and thyme.

– Add cherries to this very fragrant soup. Cool soup and refrigerate.

– Spoon into 6 small, decorative bowls, and add a dollop of sorbet, ice cream, or mascarpone cheese to serve.

FOOD SOURCES: As my grandfather Clayton used to say, tart pie cherries are as rare as hen's teeth. A good friend of mine, Ruth Eliel, begins foraging for these in early June at Armenian markets, where a few boxes of the real thing may be sold. Scout, grab, and buy. Makrut limes and leaves are available at most Asian markets, including 168 Market, H Mart, and Marukai Market.

VEGETABLE SOUP—ONE RECIPE, TEN VERSIONS

Serves 4

INGREDIENTS

1 rounded tablespoon unsalted butter or 1 tablespoon olive oil

1 onion, cut into 1/2-inch dice

1 teaspoon sugar

1 teaspoon kosher salt

1 small red or yellow waxy potato, diced into 1/2-inch cubes (omit for a lighter soup)

1 pound vegetables, washed and scrubbed or peeled as indicated:

　Carrots, cut into thick slices

　or Banana squash, peeled, cut into 1/2-inch cubes

　or Carrots, cut into thick slices, and banana squash, peeled and cut into 1/2-inch cubes

　or Sweet potatoes, peeled and cut into thick slices

　or Carrots and sweet potatoes, peeled and cut into thick slices

　or Zucchini, cut into thick slices

　or Jerusalem artichokes, scrubbed under cold water and cut into 1-inch pieces

　or Cauliflower, separated into small florets

1 quart purchased or homemade chicken broth (see page 35)

4 teaspoons chopped flat-leaf parsley, Crème Fraîche, or Pesto (see pages 38, 42)

½ cup Croutons (see page 58)

METHOD

– In a large, sturdy saucepan or Le Creuset-style soup pot, melt butter or olive oil.

– Add onion, sugar, and salt; cook slowly over medium-low heat, about 10 to 15 minutes, until onions are translucent and beginning to turn golden.

– Add potato, if desired, and vegetables of your choice; cook another 10 minutes.

– In a medium pan, heat chicken or vegetable stock, then add it to the soup pot. Continue cooking on low heat for 20 to 30 minutes.

– When the vegetables are soft, use a slotted spoon to transfer all solids to a blender. Add ½ cup or more broth and process until all solids are puréed. Return purée to broth, stirring until incorporated. You can use an immersion blender in the soup pot.

– Ladle soup into 4 bowls, adding parsley, Crème Fraîche, or Pesto; top with Croutons.

TRY THIS: In a small bowl, soften 2 tablespoons tamarind paste in 1 tablespoon hot water. Stir until tamarind is liquefied, then strain through a sieve to remove seeds. Add tamarind to the onions when they are translucent. Omit salt. Or, add lemongrass and ginger for a bright, floral undertone to the carrot, squash, or zucchini soups. Cut 2 inches of peeled ginger into large slices. Add to onions and continue cooking until onions are translucent. Remove ginger. Meanwhile, add a 4-inch piece of peeled lemongrass to the broth and heat for 10 minutes. Remove lemongrass; use broth as directed.

FOOD SOURCES: Visiting Cookbook, La Mayordomia Market, or your local farmers' market will vastly improve this recipe. The quality of the vegetables translates into gorgeously flavored soup. Try Atwater Village, Hollywood, or Pasadena Certified farmers' markets—all held on the weekend—and enjoy a dose of happy community.

Carrot Soup, one of ten variations of Vegetable Soup.

Pasta, Rice, and Legumes

Robin Koda of Koda Farms, at the Hollywood Farmers' Market. Her family has been growing heirloom rice in California's San Joaquin Valley since 1928.

CUT PASTA DOUGH

This recipe is courtesy of chef and teacher Francesca Mallus, who was born and raised in Sardinia, Italy. Francesca uses a KitchenAid stand mixer with a pasta attachment, but pasta machines, both hand-cranked and motorized, are widely available. Some roll and cut pasta dough by hand; I leave this method to the pastry experts. I often divide the dough ball in half to knead; this dough is tough.

Serves 4 to 6

INGREDIENTS
8½ ounces (250 grams) semolina
8½ ounces (250 grams) oo flour or all-purpose flour
5 pinches salt
5 eggs
5 tablespoons olive oil
Water (a splash only, if needed)

METHOD
– Place all dry ingredients into the bowl of a stand mixer with a pasta-roller attachment or in a large bowl.

– In a separate small bowl, mix eggs and olive oil. Add the wet to the dry ingredients.

– Using the dough hook, beat slowly for 1 to 2 minutes, until ingredients are combined, or mix vigorously by hand. Add scant amount of water if needed. Remove dough.

– Knead dough for about 10 minutes, until gluten is formed. The dough will become smooth rather than raggedy, and bounce back when pressed lightly with your finger. Or try the windowpane test: Roll out a small piece of dough and stretch it until you can see through it. Dough should not tear.

– Wrap dough in plastic wrap and refrigerate for at least 20 minutes or up to 2 days.

– Cut dough into quarters and stretch each section into an oblong shape. Wrap the yet-to-be-used sections in plastic to avoid drying out the dough.

– Flour your work surface. Make sure both sides of the dough are floured lightly. I just place the dough on the floured surface; if it moves easily, it is ready to be rolled.

– Begin feeding the first oblong through the pasta-roller attachment on the stand mixer, or through a pasta machine, beginning with setting 1, then repeating with settings 2, 3, and 4. Lay out flattened pasta on parchment paper.

– Switch out pasta roller for the pasta cutter, thick or thin size. Feed pasta sheets through the cutter; hang pasta on a drying rack. Repeat with remaining dough.

– To cook, prepare a large pot of boiling water with enough salt to taste "of the sea." Cook until al dente (still a bit chewy), about 3 to 4 minutes. Avoid overcooking.

– Remove pasta with a large slotted spoon. Be sure to reserve a bit of the pasta water; the starch in the water helps bind any sauce you use. Never rinse pasta!

– Serve with sauce of your choice, including Francesca's Tomato Sauce (see page 125).

FOOD SOURCES: Semolina and oo flour are available at Italian specialty markets, such as Claro's Italian Markets, Eagle Rock Italian Bakery and Deli, Roma Italian Deli and Grocery, and Truffle Brothers.

FILLED PASTA DOUGH Including Ravioli, Tortellini, and Tortelloni

This recipe is courtesy of chef and teacher Francesca Mallus, born and raised in Sardinia, Italy, and a specialist in Italian and Mediterranean food—including pasta! Because there are no eggs in this dough, it is very, very delicate and so is not rolled as thinly as some. This is the first part of a multi-step process, so I often prepare the dough the night before. See Ricotta Filling for Tortellini (see page 124) for one way to cut, fill, and shape this very versatile pasta.

Serves 4 to 6

INGREDIENTS

8 ounces semolina flour
2½ ounces oo flour or all-purpose flour
2 generous pinches sea salt or kosher salt
3 tablespoons olive oil
5½ ounces water

METHOD

– Place semolina, oo or all-purpose flour, and salt in the bowl of a stand mixer or other large bowl.

– Whisk olive oil and water in a small bowl. Add wet ingredients to the dry ingredients.

– Using the dough-hook attachment, beat slowly 1 to 2 minutes until ingredients are combined. Or you can stir vigorously with a large spoon until combined. Scrape sides of bowl with a rubber spatula to ensure that all dry ingredients are incorporated.

– Remove dough (it should form a loose ball).

– Knead dough for about 10 minutes, until gluten is formed. As you knead, the dough will become smooth; it is ready when it bounces back when pressed lightly with your finger. Or try the windowpane test: Stretch a small piece of dough with your fingers until you can see through it. If it does not tear, the gluten is sufficient.

– Wrap dough tightly in plastic wrap and refrigerate for 20 minutes or up to 3 days.

– Cut dough into quarters and stretch each section into an oblong shape. Wrap the yet-to-be-used sections in plastic to avoid drying out the dough.

– Flour only one side of the dough, as you will want the other side to stay tacky for filling and then forming into your choice of pasta shape.

– Begin feeding dough through the pasta-roller attachment of a stand mixer or through a pasta machine, beginning with setting 1, then repeating with setting 2 and 3. If I am feeling dexterous, I will roll the dough once more on setting 4, so that it becomes translucent, for a more refined pasta. This requires skill, as the dough is delicate.

– As you complete the pasta, place the lengths on parchment paper to avoid sticking; cover with plastic to keep strips from drying out.

– If dough becomes too long to handle, cut it in half before completing the rolling.

– Cut dough to the shape and size desired and fill.

FOOD SOURCES: Semolina and oo flour are readily available at Italian specialty markets, such as Claro's Italian Markets, Eagle Rock Italian Bakery and Deli, Roma Italian Deli and Grocery, and Truffle Brothers.

RICOTTA TORTELLINI

This delicious and simple recipe is courtesy of chef and teacher Francesca Mallus.

Serves 4 to 6

INGREDIENTS

Filled Pasta Dough (see page 122)
7 ounces fresh ricotta cheese
1 egg yolk
3 tablespoons grated cheese (pecorino or parmesan)
Pinch saffron
Kosher salt to taste
4 quarts of water

METHOD

– Roll out pasta dough, a quarter of the dough at a time; then cut into 3-inch circles.

– In a small bowl, combine remaining ingredients and taste. Add more salt if necessary.

– Spoon ½ teaspoon or more of ricotta filling into the center of each circle. Do not overfill, or you will not be able to close the tortellini without making a mess.

– Fold dough over filling and seal tightly by pressing with your fingers to make a half moon. Draw the angled edges together and crimp to create the bonnet shape. Place finished tortellini on a parchment-covered half-sheet baking pan. Continue filling until dough is used.

– Fill a large pot with 4 quarts of water and enough salt to "taste of the sea," about 4 tablespoons; bring to a boil. Add all tortellini and cook until they float, about 3 to 4 minutes.

– Remove tortellini with a slotted spoon. Serve with Francesca's Tomato Sauce (see recipe facing page), Classic Pesto (see page 42), or any other preferred sauce.

FRANCESCA'S TOMATO SAUCE

Another of Francesca Mallus's recipes, for which I am eternally grateful.

Serves 4 to 6

INGREDIENTS

1 tablespoon extra-virgin olive oil
1 large clove garlic, coarsely chopped
1 pound tomatoes, coarsely chopped
2 whole sun-dried tomatoes, coarsely chopped
Pinch saffron
1 cup water
Fresh basil or oregano (3 large leaves basil, thinly sliced; or a sprig of oregano, chopped)
Kosher salt to taste

METHOD

– Heat olive oil in a heavy-bottomed saucepan over medium-high heat. Add chopped garlic and cook for 3 to 5 minutes. When garlic is golden brown, add fresh and dried tomatoes and saffron. Cook mixture, covered, for 10 minutes. Add 1 cup water and continue to cook for another 10 minutes.

– About 2 minutes before sauce is done, add the basil or oregano. Add salt to taste.

– Use an immersion blender to combine all ingredients into a slightly chunky sauce.

FOOD SOURCES: It pays to go the Italian specialty-store route. Claro's Italian Markets, Eagle Rock Italian Bakery and Deli, Roma Italian Deli and Grocery, and Truffle Brothers are all great places to purchase good-quality cheese and sun-dried tomatoes. Indian food markets often carry excellent saffron.

PASTA WITH COUNTRY-STYLE PESTO

Warning: This is not a diet food, but it is so easy and so, so good!

Serves 4

INGREDIENTS

2 tablespoons salt

Country-Style Pesto (see page 42)

1 pound good-quality pasta (best to use durum wheat pasta with texture that allows sauce to cling) or Cut Pasta Dough (see page 121)

2 tablespoons butter

½ pound parmesan cheese, freshly grated, divided (it will fluff up and look like a lot)

METHOD

– Fill a 6-quart saucepan three-quarters full with water, and add salt. Heat to boiling.

– Add pasta, reduce heat when water returns to a boil, and cook pasta until al dente. Drain, but do not rinse. You will want the starch to remain on the pasta, as it will help thicken the sauce.

– Return pasta to the saucepan; add butter and stir. Then add pesto and half of the parmesan. Stir to combine.

– Serve hot with remaining parmesan on the side.

FOOD SOURCES: Basil is best purchased in season (spring through summer) at farmers' markets. For ready-made pasta, try Claro's Italian Markets, Roma Italian Deli and Grocery, Semolina Artisanal Pasta, or Surfas Culinary District.

MACARONI AND CHEESE

We served this at our daughter Nori and son-in-law Anthony's wedding after a gourmet catered meal. It was late, there was dancing, and this was a welcome bit of comfort food.

Serves 4 to 6

Preheat oven to 350°.

INGREDIENTS

2¼ cups whole milk
¼ cup (½ stick) unsalted butter, plus more for topping
1 to 3 tablespoons flour, plus more as needed to thicken
A few gratings fresh whole nutmeg
Large pinch cayenne pepper
1 teaspoon kosher salt
Freshly ground black pepper
1 pound jack cheese, grated, divided
½ to ⅔ pound good-quality gruyère cheese, shredded, divided
16 ounces pasta (macaroni, penne, rigatoni, or orecchiette)
1 cup fresh breadcrumbs or panko

METHOD

– In a small saucepan over low heat, warm milk to a simmer and set aside.

– Melt ¼ cup butter in a large saucepan over low heat.

– When butter starts to foam, add 1 tablespoon flour at a time, stirring after each addition, until mixture slightly thickens. Cook for 1 minute or more to make a roux.

– Cook until the roux is golden brown and nutty smelling.

– Slowly pour heated milk into roux, whisking constantly over medium-low heat; cook until mixture bubbles and becomes thick, about 5 minutes. (To avoid lumps, add a small amount of milk to roux until it has become a thick sauce, then add remaining milk.)

– Add nutmeg, cayenne pepper, salt, and pepper.

– Slowly stir in grated jack and gruyère cheese, reserving about 1/3 cup of each for the topping.

– Cook milk and cheese mixture over low heat until cheese is melted, another 2 minutes or so; set aside.

– Cook pasta according to directions but for slightly less time than is indicated on the package, as the pasta will continue to cook when it is baked with the cheese sauce.

– Drain pasta; stir into cheese sauce and pour into a large buttered, heat-proof baking pan (rectangle or oval).

– Top with breadcrumbs and reserved grated cheese and butter. Bake for about 20 minutes, until bubbling and cooked hot all the way through. Serve immediately.

TRY THIS: I substitute an equivalent amount of leftover cheeses, as long as they are not too boldly flavored. For other toppings, add ½ cup finely diced and fried pancetta to 1 tablespoon chopped parsley, ½ cup panko, and ½ cup grated parmesan cheese.

THREE-MUSHROOM RISOTTO

Serves 4

INGREDIENTS

Large handful dried mushrooms (shiitake or porcini are fine)
2 to 3 tablespoons butter
1 pound fresh portobello and cremini mushrooms, finely sliced
1 cup arborio, carnaroli, or Koda Farms Kokuho Rose rice
4 cups chicken broth, or more—best is homemade (see pages 34 and 35)
½ to 1 cup dry white wine—good-quality
About 1 cup freshly grated parmesan cheese
Kosher salt to taste

METHOD

– Soak dried mushrooms in hot water for about 15 minutes.

– Add butter to a large, straight-sided sauté pan and heat over medium heat until foamy.

– Add fresh mushrooms to hot butter and cook until soft and slightly browned, about 10 minutes. Remove mushrooms and set aside.

– Add 1 cup rice to sauté pan and brown slightly.

– In a separate large cooking pot, heat 4 cups chicken broth to a simmer over low heat.

– Pour about ½ cup wine over sautéed rice.

– When wine is absorbed, pour 1 ladle of hot chicken broth over rice and stir until absorbed. Continue until the rice is al dente. Drain rehydrated mushrooms through a sieve, reserving the mushroom liquid. (The sieve will catch any debris from the dried mushrooms.)

– Add a small amount of mushroom liquid to risotto.

– Add a bit more wine to taste. Add all mushrooms and mix into the rice.

– Add about ½ cup cheese to saucepan for flavor. Do not add salt until you have added the parmesan, as it may be salty enough. Serve with additional parmesan on the side.

TRY THIS: Zucchini, yellow squash, or any seasonal vegetable may be substituted. Chop coarsely and sauté in butter as for the mushrooms.

FOOD SOURCES: For mushrooms, Cookbook, farmers' markets; for rice, Claro's Italian Markets, Cookbook, Hollywood Farmers' Market, Roma Italian Deli and Grocery; for a good hunk of Reggiano-Parmigiano cheese, Claro's Italian Markets, Roma Italian Deli and Grocery.

MINH'S VEGAN PORRIDGE WITH SPRING GREEN SAUCE

There is a pattern for porridge. It always includes rice or grains, flavored broth, and toppings. Variations are endless but depend on attention to tastes that resonate and the seasonal availability of ingredients. This porridge draws on the subtlety and quality of ingredients such as Koda Farms Heirloom Rice and sweet spring or filtered water, and is finished with Negi Oil (see page 48) and Geranium Pickled Baby Onions (see page 51).

Serves 6

INGREDIENTS for Porridge

4 cups filtered water, room temperature
1 cup rice (medium-grain Koda Farms Heirloom Kokuho Rose is a favorite)
3 stalks lemongrass, peeled and cut into 4 pieces per stalk
4 inches ginger, peeled, cut into 1-inch pieces, and bruised
4 to 5 small shallots, peeled and cut in half
2 generous pinches kosher salt (Minh prefers Jacobsen's)

METHOD

– Add water, rice, lemongrass, ginger, shallots, and a pinch of salt to a 4-quart saucepan. If you start with hot water, the rice will lose its integrity. To make porridge, rice is not washed; the starch is what creates the sauce-like texture.

– Bring to a boil over high heat, then reduce heat to medium-low and continue simmering for 1 hour or more. Stir infrequently, as you want to avoid mushiness.

– The porridge is done when its texture is creamy and thick. The rice will be al dente, similar to risotto. You can add a little more water to retain a risotto-like consistency.

– Remove the ginger, shallots, and lemongrass. Add another pinch of salt.

INGREDIENTS for Spring Green Sauce

1 bunch cilantro, stems and leaves
1 bunch green or Negi onions, green section only
5 to 6 fennel fronds
14 ounces 100% coconut milk
A few leaves baby spinach, chard, and parsley

METHOD

– Place all ingredients into a blender; blend on the highest setting until smooth.

TO SERVE

Ladle porridge into shallow soup bowls. Add a swirl of Spring Green Sauce and Negi Oil and a few slices of Geranium Pickled Baby Onions.

TRY THIS: For a more robust version of porridge, roast rice or grain in butter, use chicken broth instead of water, and add richer toppings, such as braised short ribs and caramelized vegetables.

FOOD SOURCES: Koda Farms for rice, Thao Family Farm for lemongrass and ginger, T & D Farms for shallots. These providers are at the Hollywood Farmers' Market.

Minh's unusual and delicious amaranth flower tempura provides a crisp contrast to her Vegan Porridge with Spring Green Sauce. Minh's tempura batter is made from two simple ingredients: Koda Farms rice flour and carbonated water. The petal-like and delicious garnish is Geranium Pickled Baby Onions (see page 51).

BLACK RICE WITH MAKRUT LIME LEAVES

Excellent with barbecued ribs, chicken, and other richly flavored meats.

Serves 4

INGREDIENTS

1 tablespoon butter
2 shallots, finely chopped
6 to 8 makrut lime leaves
½ to 1 teaspoon kosher salt
¼ Meyer lemon, thinly sliced
Handful golden raisins
1½ cups black rice
3 cups homemade chicken broth
¼ cup shredded sweet coconut
Handful peanuts (leave out if having company; a lot of people are allergic)

METHOD

– Melt butter in a 3-quart pan.

– Add shallots, lime leaves, salt, lemon slices, and raisins to pan. Cook over low heat, stirring frequently as the shallots caramelize.

– Add rice and cook 5 minutes more.

– In the meantime, in a smaller pan, heat chicken broth until almost boiling. Add to rice mixture, bring to a boil, and reduce heat to a low simmer. Cover and cook for 35 to 40 minutes, then remove cover and continue cooking on medium heat until all liquid is absorbed. Remove lime leaves.

– Add coconut and peanuts (if using), stir to fluff, cook a bit longer, and serve.

NOTE: I use the sweetened variety of coconut that can be found in the baking section of most supermarkets. It adds a great deal of taste to the dish.

FOOD SOURCES: 168 Market, Bhanu Indian Grocery and Cuisine, Cookbook, H Mart, Namaste Spiceland, Punjab Indian Grocery, Surfas Culinary District.

"The flavor was excellent and brought out the lovely chewiness of the black rice. The Meyer lemon was delicious, and the lime leaves were interesting and fresh-tasting. The color is striking and exotic, and would dress up a simply prepared protein." NORIKO GAMBLIN, *sophisticated and adventurous cook, recipe tester*

FRIED RICE

From the YWCA of Kuala Lumpur cooking class circa 1966. When I was a young teen, I had the great fortune of living overseas with my father and stepmother in the Philippines and Malaysia. My father was a country director for the Peace Corps, and these years were some of my happiest. I learned the joy of unrestrained exploration of extraordinary images, cultures, languages, and food, and my confidence grew as I navigated each country. My parents supported my growing independence, allowing me to travel alone, volunteer at an indigenous hospital, and participate as a Girl Guide on a remote camping trip in the jungles of Malaysia.

Serves 6 to 8

INGREDIENTS

4 cups cooked long-grain rice

3 tablespoons vegetable or canola oil

2 to 3 cloves garlic, smashed flat with a knife

2-inch section ginger, peeled and thinly sliced

3 carrots, thinly sliced on the diagonal

1 pound Chinese-style barbecued pork, Chasu Pork (see facing page), or lap cheong
   Chinese sausage, thinly sliced

15-ounce can bamboo shoots, drained, thoroughly rinsed, and thinly sliced (optional)

About 3 tablespoons soy sauce

1 bunch green onions, thinly sliced

1 egg, scrambled and fried in a nonstick pan to a thin sheet, then sliced into ribbons

METHOD

– Spread rice onto half-sheet pan and let sit at least 30 minutes or overnight.

– In a wok or large frying pan over high heat, add oil, garlic, and ginger. Fry until oil is fragrant and garlic and ginger are golden brown.

– Remove garlic and ginger from pan to cool. Finely chop both and set aside.

– Heat oil in wok and add carrots; stir-fry until al dente. Add pork and bamboo shoots; stir-fry until warmed through.

– Add rice in small batches, allowing the hot oil to coat.

– Add soy sauce to flavor and moisten. Taste as you go, to avoid over-salting.

– Continue stir-frying until flavors are combined.

– Turn onto a large platter. Add green onions and egg ribbons. Sprinkle with fried chopped garlic and ginger.

Serve with Taka's Pickles or Margie's Sweet and Sour Cucumbers (see pages 53 and 54).

NOTE: This recipe requires up to two days to prepare, but is relatively easy once you have made the various components: Chasu Pork, pickles, and rice.

"You were right. This recipe was a bit more difficult than the others. I took your advice and simplified it. I used Margie's Sweet and Sour Cucumbers and bought Chinese pork instead of making it. I added green onions, egg, and ginger. I did not use carrots."
ESTHER KANG, *novice cook, self-described millennial, recipe tester*

CHASU PORK

A centerpiece of Fried Rice, but great on its own.

Serves 6 to 8 for Fried Rice, serves 2 to 3 as a main dish

Preheat oven to 375°.

INGREDIENTS

1 medium pork tenderloin (about 1 pound)
About ½ cup hoisin sauce
3 to 5 cloves garlic, peeled and cut lengthwise in half or thirds, depending on size

METHOD

– Remove white membrane of the tenderloin—"silver skin"—by slipping a paring knife between the silver skin and muscle fibers. Angle the knife slightly upward and use a gentle back-and-forth sawing action. It should come off easily.

– Make slight cuts in pork and push in garlic slivers.

– Use a sharp knife to cut a shallow criss-cross pattern on all sides of the tenderloin.

– Brush hoisin sauce over the entire tenderloin, reserving a little to add halfway through cooking. Place tenderloin on baking rack set in a shallow pan.

– Bake for about 30 minutes, until pork is cooked but still pink to maintain moistness (about 145° on an instant-read thermometer).

FOOD SOURCES: For most ingredients, including Chinese-style barbecued pork, 168 Market and H Mart. For the pork tenderloin, Armen Market, Schriner's Fine Sausages, Sprouts Farmers Market.

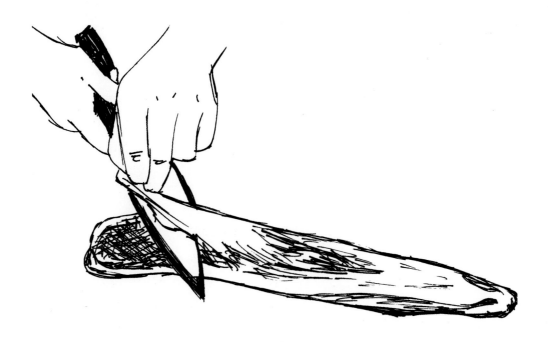

ERIC'S ANASAZI CHILE BEANS

On a recent trip to southern Utah, we acquired a 10-pound bag of beans. Dubbed "Anasazi" beans because they come by way of the old Pueblo native culture, they turned out to be exceptionally fresh and so rehydrated easily and cooked quickly. These beans have a lovely creamy texture and satisfying flavor. The lesson is to avoid beans that have been sitting on the grocer's shelf, and pay a bit more for fresh.

Here is Eric's recipe for beans in a chile sauce that borrows a special addition, honey, from the New Mexican dish carne adovada.

Serves 8

INGREDIENTS

1½ cups dried beans, such as pinto
1 small onion, finely diced
1 fresh pasilla or similar green chile, finely diced
2 teaspoons oil
1 dried chile, such as ancho, finely diced
2 teaspoons cumin seeds, freshly ground
2 tablespoons medium chili powder
2½ teaspoons dried Mexican oregano or 2 teaspoons regular oregano
¾ teaspoon salt
1½ teaspoons honey

METHOD

– Wash beans, place in 3-quart saucepan, cover with water 1 inch above beans, and leave to soak 6 to 24 hours. The longer they soak, the faster they'll cook and the creamier they'll be. Cook soaked beans very slowly over low heat, without salt, until the individual beans are softening but still al dente, about 1½ hours, depending on freshness of beans.

– In a small frying pan, sauté onion and chiles in oil until soft, about 10 minutes.

– Place ground cumin seeds in a small bowl. Add chili powder, oregano, and salt. When the beans are nearly done, add the sautéed mixture, dry ingredients, and honey. If necessary, add more water so that mixture is slightly soupy. Simmer for another 30 to 40 minutes. The beans should be soft and the flavors in the sauce integrated.

FOOD SOURCES: Cookbook and Surfas Culinary District for Rancho Gordo beans (a very good product). For chiles and beans, Grand Central Market, La Mayordomia Market, El Mercado de Los Angeles, Super A Foods, Super King Markets, Vallarta Supermarkets, farmers' markets.

"For Armenians, the kitchen is the ultimate center of family life, growing out of scarcity and dislocation. Each encounter on my parents' long journey to a new home added something to their palate. At our restaurant in Altadena, we served black beans and rice and fresh yellowtail and tahini tacos, along with more traditional Armenian fare such as dolma and tabbouleh." Jack Aghoian with his parents, Mary and Abraham Aghoian, in their Altadena garden.

JACK AGHOIAN

When a family's history is one of displacement and immigration, what can be carried is memory. For Jack Aghoian's family, these memories take their most tangible form in its love of food. Jack's parents, Mary and Abraham, spent their youth in Syria and Cuba, respectively, as each of these countries welcomed Armenian refugees. Mary grew up in the small village of Kessab, in northwestern Syria. Meat was scarce, and Mary's mother, Ovsanna, learned to extend protein by adding cracked wheat and onions while relying on a primarily vegetarian diet. Abraham's family put down roots in Cuba, where black beans and rice became family staples.

Fast-forward several years. Mary and Abraham found themselves in Lebanon in 1961, where Mary was working as a ground hostess for Egyptian Airlines, and Abraham was searching for relatives who were said to have relocated to Lebanon from Turkey. Instead, he met Mary, and after a seventeen-day courtship proposed marriage. Immediately afterward, the couple immigrated to the United States, settling in Pasadena, where Abraham's sister and brother-in-law had created a home. Mary began a long career as a community liaison specialist for the local school district, working with newly arrived immigrants. Abraham's independent streak motivated him to open a restaurant, Aghoian's Dining Room. "I didn't know how to cook," he says, "but Mary did." She instructed her willing husband in everything she had absorbed from her childhood in Kessab, where all food was made from scratch. Her know-how served the Aghoians well.

In the early 1970s there was only one small Armenian market in the area. Jack's memories of the family's commitment to serving high-quality, authentic Armenian food inspired an example of foraging that few can top. He describes caravanning with two or three families to harvest olives in nearby Santa Clarita and to pick grape leaves in Fresno. The Aghoians preserved the olives and the grape leaves in salt and stored both treasures in large crocks in their basement. Jack describes growing up in the restaurant, bussing, cleaning, and prepping. By the age of nine he boasted excellent knife skills. When Abraham was ready to retire, he offered Jack the opportunity to take over the business. Shortly thereafter, Jack the university student became Jack the restaurant owner, renaming his establishment Jack's Kasbah. Many of the recipes continued as staples—most notably the family's Yogurt Soup, or Madzooneh Shorba (see page 113)—but Jack's concern for healthy eating meant lighter fare, and his love for a variety of food cultures led to the inclusion of Peruvian, Japanese, and Mexican dishes on the menu.

Although Jack sold the restaurant, later owned by Alta Eats chef Paul Ragan, he can be found at his own kitchen stove every day. "Cooking to me is like breathing," he says. A consummate food maker, his sense-filled memories fuel his fascination for all things edible. A favorite story hearkens back to the time when eleven-year-old Jack visited Kessab to experience his mother's early history. "There were these Kurdish women baking flatbread over an open fire. They had been cooking tomatoes on a slow hearth all day, until the tomatoes had turned to paste. One of the women gave me a slice of warm bread spread with this paste. I never forgot it, sitting on the wall of some ruins, eating exquisite food. I guess I am always chasing flavor."

Baklava
Jack makes his own, of course; he describes it as very light.

Café au lait
Jack and his sister Rosette's paternal grand-mother, Vartanoush, made this after-school treat daily.

Cuban beans and rice
An Aghoian family staple, a tangible memory of Jack's father's early years in Cuba.

Grape leaves
When Armenian grocery stores were scarce in the 1970s, Jack's family traveled to Fresno to pick their own grape leaves.

Aghoian Family Yogurt
Made daily; the foundation of many Aghoian family dishes (see page 40).

Olives
The Aghoians foraged for olives near Santa Clarita and brined their own when Jack was a boy.

Peruvian tamales
Jack's wife is Peruvian, sufficient reason to master yet another cuisine.

The Menu
The variations of the Aghoian Altadena restaurants share a history of nearly thirty years.

Stews and casseroles, zucchini and eggplant
Jack's maternal grandmother, Ovsanna, stretched meat by creating stews and casseroles of cracked wheat and vegetables.

Lakhannaeh Sarma
A delicious variation on dolma, the flavorful rice filling is wrapped in cabbage or swiss chard.

Sushi
One of Jack's favorite foods; he learned to prepare his own sushi rice and fish.

Home-baked flatbread with tomato paste
This beautifully simple dish tasted in Syria may be Jack's strongest, most evocative food memory.

Madzooneh Shorba
A signature soup from Jack's restaurant days: Yogurt Soup (see page 113).

Salads and Vegetables with Taste

Marta Teegen, co-owner of Cookbook with husband, Robert Stelzner, in the couple's Highland Park store. Marta's many years of farming are reflected in her love of high-quality produce.

QUICK GUACAMOLE

My guacamole is admittedly gringo, as one of its key ingredients is ready-made Sriracha sauce, now as ubiquitous as ketchup once was.

Makes about 1½ cups

INGREDIENTS

3 ripe but not too soft Haas avocados (these have a textured, dark skin and are quite dense and flavorful)
Squeeze of fresh lemon juice and kosher salt to taste (start with just a bit—it is easy to oversalt or make the guacamole too sour)
1 large clove garlic, pressed
½ to 1 teaspoon Sriracha Hot Chili Sauce (do not use the version with garlic)

METHOD

– Peel the avocados, place in a medium bowl, and mash with a fork.

– Add lemon juice, salt, garlic, and chile sauce to taste, adding more of any of the last 3 ingredients if needed (but just very small amounts).

– Mix until completely combined.

MONICA'S GUACAMOLE

This is the real deal, more complex in taste and a bit more time-consuming than my version. Mario Rodriguez's wife, Monica, and I made the guacamole together, reverse engineering to create the recipe. Taste as you go, just like we did; it's a hallmark of all great cooks. If you prefer less or more heat, adjust the amount of jalapeño.

Makes about 1½ cups

INGREDIENTS

2 large avocados (thin-skinned Fuerte is Monica and Mario's favorite, but Haas is also fine)
1 small tomato, seeded and finely diced (about ½ cup)
⅓ medium white onion, finely diced (about ¼ cup)
1 medium jalapeño, very finely diced (remove seeds if you are sensitive to heat)
¼ cup finely chopped cilantro
Juice of 1½ large limes
1 tablespoon salt

METHOD

– In a medium bowl, mash avocados.

– Add tomato, onion, jalapeño, and cilantro, and combine.

– Add lime juice and salt (begin with ½ tablespoon salt, tasting as you go).

FOOD SOURCES: La Mayordomia Market, El Mercado de Los Angeles, Super A Foods, Vallarta Supermarkets, farmers' markets.

PICKLED COLESLAW

Serves 6

INGREDIENTS

1 small head white cabbage (about 1½ pounds)
¼ cup kosher salt
10 cups warm water
¼ cup apple cider vinegar
¼ cup grapeseed oil or other neutral oil
1 tablespoon sugar
1 clove garlic, pressed
20 grinds black pepper

METHOD

– With a large chef's knife, cut cabbage in half and remove core.

– Finely slice cabbage (less than ¼ inch), or use the slicing blade of a food processor.

– Add salt to a large bowl. Cover with warm water (about 10 cups) and mix with a spoon or your hand until salt is dissolved. Add cabbage.

– Marinate cabbage mixture for at least 3 hours or overnight.

– Drain cabbage thoroughly, squeeze out excess liquid, and taste to ensure it has a salty tang.

– In a small bowl, mix the remaining ingredients to create a vinaigrette. Pour over cabbage.

– Allow coleslaw to rest at least 3 hours before serving.

NOTE: The coleslaw should taste very salty after its saltwater soak. Do not worry; it will taste delicious once it marinates.

"This dish is a breeze to prepare and more than worth the minimal effort."
NORIKO GAMBLIN, *sophisticated and adventurous cook, recipe tester*

Elegant Leftovers: THREE SALADES COMPOSÉES

Composed salads are made of leftovers repurposed so cleverly that they look fresh and taste delicious.

SALAD

Dress a generous amount of greens with any of the basic salad dressings (see pages 45 and 46). Arrange dressed greens on a large platter and add any of the suggested toppings. I often place each ingredient in a thick stripe—it is prettier. My good friend Barbara thinks it is a bit obsessive.

TOPPING ONE

Sliced leftover chicken breast
Chickpeas, drained and rinsed
Cubed leftover beets
Crumbled leftover bacon
Crumbled blue cheese
Sliced roasted almonds
Deviled eggs

ANOTHER TOPPING

Sliced leftover steak (flank or tri-tip)
Sliced tomatoes
Pickled Mushrooms (see page 152)
Thinly sliced parmesan cheese
Sliced cooked carrots

OR ANOTHER TOPPING

Crumbled feta cheese
Sliced leftover steak or turkey
Cherry tomatoes
Chickpeas, drained and rinsed
Thinly sliced cucumbers
Potato salad

TRY THIS: There are many more ideas: Use your basic leftovers, add some cheese, and enjoy with a hot roll or baguette and butter. The dressed greens add a great deal of flavor to the salad, but it is a good idea to provide a side bowl of vinaigrette with the toppings, if you wish.

FOOD SOURCES: The better the ingredients—including fresh vegetables—the tastier your salad will be. Invest in quality produce at markets such as Cookbook, H Mart, La Mayordomia, Super King, and farmers' markets. Shop for cheeses at specialty stores, such as The Cheese Cave, Milkfarm, Nicole's Market & Café, and Say Cheese.

MARINATED KALE SALAD

This is a delicious salad and very easy to assemble. I like it because it can be made ahead, as early as the morning of the day you serve it. The kale becomes much more flavorful when it marinates throughout the day.

Serves 4

INGREDIENTS

Walnut or Hazelnut Dressing (see page 46); omit the nuts.

1 large bunch curly kale, washed, dried, and sliced very thinly. Cut the rib out of each leaf before slicing.

1 large shallot, sliced very thinly

1 large handful dried cranberries

1 large handful almonds, blanched, toasted, and sliced

Add-ins: sliced avocado or grated manchego cheese

METHOD

– Make the dressing.

– Combine kale, shallot, and cranberries in a large bowl.

– Add the dressing, and mix. Be generous with the amount, as the kale actually soaks up the dressing as it softens.

– Let sit for at least 3 hours on the counter.

– Just before serving, add nuts and avocado or cheese; toss again.

FOOD SOURCES: Kale is an all-purpose plant that is exceedingly easy to grow through the cooler months and can also handle our sudden heat spells. Its popularity waxes and wanes, but when combined with bold flavors, it is delicious. Cookbook sells a large variety of beautiful kale, and it is a regular at farmers' markets.

WINTER SALAD

Ricotta salata cheese, thinly sliced (use a vegetable peeler for extra-thin slices)

Toasted walnuts, toasted hazelnuts, or toasted sliced almonds

Dried cranberries and blueberries

Arugula and mixed greens from the farmers' market

Lightly toss with Walnut or Hazelnut Dressing (see page 46)

SYLVIA'S PICKLED MUSHROOMS

Sylvia Lefton, my oldest and dearest friend Barbara's mother, was an amazing cook and often invited me to share meals with her family—lucky me! These mushrooms were added to a simple green salad.

Makes ½ to 1 quart

INGREDIENTS

⅓ cup tarragon vinegar or sherry vinegar with a sprig of fresh tarragon

¼ cup oil (any kind of vegetable or grapeseed oil will do, although olive oil tends to become solid in the refrigerator, so I would avoid this)

1 medium clove garlic, crushed

1½ teaspoons sugar

1 tablespoon water

¾ teaspoon salt

Freshly ground pepper, a few grinds

Dash hot sauce, such as Tabasco

1 small onion, thinly sliced, and rings separated

1 pound small fresh mushroom caps, stems removed and reserved for another use; quarter if large

METHOD

– Combine vinegar, oil, garlic, sugar, water, salt, pepper, and hot sauce in a bowl.

– Place onion and mushrooms in a glass quart jar.

– Pour in marinade and let sit at room temperature at least 1 hour. I invert the jar a few times during the hour to better distribute the vinaigrette.

– Refrigerate at least 8 hours before serving. Keeps 1 to 2 weeks in the refrigerator.

CORN WITH MASCARPONE

Serves 6 to 8

INGREDIENTS

6 to 8 ears fresh corn, shucked and corn silk removed
½ cup (1 stick) unsalted butter
2 tablespoons olive oil
Kosher salt and freshly ground pepper
3 tablespoons mascarpone cheese, more if desired
Pinch ground paprika—sweet or hot

METHOD

– Remove corn kernels (a messy job) by first cutting about ½ inch off the pointed end of the corn ear to make sure it is stable. Stand corn on cut end. Then slide a sharp knife down sides of each ear of corn until all kernels are cut off. Be careful; it is easy for the knife to slip.

– Place kernels in a bowl and remove any remaining strands of corn silk.

– Add butter and olive oil to a large sauté pan; heat over medium-low heat until foamy.

– Pour kernels into sauté pan. Cook until corn begins to be fragrant; add salt and pepper. Taste for seasoning.

– When corn is heated through and turns a darker yellow, add mascarpone cheese.

– Cook until cheese is incorporated and heated through.

– Pour mixture into serving bowl and sprinkle a pinch of paprika over the top.

JACK'S LAKHANNAEH SARMA (VEGETARIAN CABBAGE ROLLS)

Jack Aghoian departs from the more traditional wrapping of grape leaves in this delicious and very healthy dish. Jack's beautiful cabbage-rolling technique requires practice; he's been doing it since he was a little boy. The rice is cooked in a two-step process.

Serves 12 to 15 (may be reduced by half)

INGREDIENTS

2 medium heads cabbage, cored (avoid large cabbage heads, as their ribs are too large)

3 tablespoons salt, divided

3 medium onions, finely chopped

5 cloves garlic, peeled and finely chopped

2 cups rice (long-grain, such as basmati; or parboiled, such as Uncle Ben's)

2 heaping tablespoons tomato paste

1 cup fresh lemon juice

1 large bunch Italian parsley, stems removed, finely chopped

2 tablespoons good-quality olive oil

METHOD

– Place cabbage in a large cooking pot, cover with water, and add 1 tablespoon salt.

– Bring to a boil over high heat, reduce heat to medium and simmer for 10 minutes. Leaves should be softened enough to roll, but not overcooked. Remove cabbage from water, cool, and carefully remove the leaves, one at a time. If inner leaves are not cooked enough, return cabbage head to boiling water for a few minutes more.

– Place onions in a large sauté pan. Cook over medium heat until translucent, about 10 minutes. Mix in garlic and rice.

– In a separate bowl, mix tomato paste with enough hot water to equal 4 cups. Add tomato paste mixture to rice mixture. Add lemon juice.

– Bring mixture to a boil, turn down heat to a simmer, and continue cooking for 5 to 8 minutes. Rice should be al dente. Remove mixture from heat and let cool.

– Add parsley and 2 tablespoons salt to cooled mixture.

– Cut a small notch out of the bottom of the rib of each cabbage leaf; set aside.

– Place a generous tablespoon of rice mixture toward the bottom of each leaf.

– Fold the notched end of the cabbage leaf over the mixture; fold the left and right sides toward the center of the leaf. Beginning from the bottom, tightly roll the cabbage leaf. (If the leaf is narrow, fold over one side only.) Place rolls into a 6-quart pot, as close together as possible, seam-side down. Make sure open ends are butted against the side of the pot or another roll to prevent filling from spilling out.

– Pour 3 cups hot water on and around cabbage rolls. Cover the pot and heat water to a boil, then reduce heat to a simmer to steam the rolls, about 20 minutes.

– Remove the cover, let the water settle to the bottom, then add olive oil.

– Return cover to the pot. Empty the pot of its liquid, holding the cabbage back with the cover. Discard the water or reserve it for soup.

TRY THIS: Any leafy vegetable works well, especially swiss chard. Place chard leaves in boiling, salted water for 2 to 3 minutes; otherwise they will become too fragile to roll.

RUMI'S SAAG (CURRIED CREAMED SPINACH)

This version of saag is prevalent in Northern Indian cuisine, where cream is often used for a richer finish. I first tasted Rumi Mahmood's version served with an exquisite plate of rice and Shrimp Dopiaza (see page 178). Rumi often uses frozen spinach, which is of excellent quality, having been flash-frozen immediately after picking. For me, it means easy access to a delicious dish. (See Rumi's profile on page 167.)

Serves 4 as a side dish

INGREDIENTS

2 tablespoons vegetable oil
1 medium onion, finely chopped
2 tablespoons ginger, chopped
3 to 4 cloves garlic, finely diced
1 teaspoon red chile flakes or cayenne
1 teaspoon ground turmeric
½ teaspoon ground cumin
½ teaspoon ground coriander
1 teaspoon salt, more if needed
12 ounces frozen spinach or 1½ pounds fresh, blanched and all water squeezed out
½ cup half-and-half or cream

METHOD

– Heat oil in a 10-inch or larger skillet over low heat. Add onion and sauté until translucent, about 10 minutes.

– Add ginger and cook for 5 minutes or more. Add the garlic and cook until fragrant, about 10 more minutes.

– Add chile flakes or cayenne, turmeric, cumin, coriander, and salt.

– Continue cooking until flavors are mellow (neither smelling nor tasting raw), about 10 more minutes.

– Add spinach and half-and-half or cream; simmer until hot, about 5 minutes.

– Blend mixture in a food processor or blender.

– Serve as a side dish with other types of main dish curries, rice, and roti or naan (flatbreads), or with Turmeric Chili Crêpes (see page 57).

TRY THIS: Saag Aloo (Spinach with Potatoes) is a common and heartier variation. Parboil 2 medium red or Yukon gold potatoes, peel, and cut into ½-inch dice. Season with salt and pepper and brown in oil. Add blended Saag to the potatoes. Heat for about 2 more minutes.

NOTE: Blanching means to briefly boil vegetables and then stop the cooking by plunging them into ice water. After blanching, always drain thoroughly by squeezing vegetables dry with a clean towel.

FENNEL GRATIN

Serves 10

Preheat oven to 400°.

INGREDIENTS

10 to 12 fennel bulbs, cut in 1-inch slices (remove stalks)
½ cup (1 stick) unsalted butter, cut into small cubes, plus extra for greasing the pan
¾ pound Taleggio or other semisoft cheese, cut into small pieces (as this is a soft
   cheese, it helps to cut it while very cold to avoid a mess)
6 ounces prosciutto, thinly sliced
½ cup freshly grated parmesan cheese, or enough to cover the top
Salt and freshly ground pepper

METHOD

– Cook fennel slices in boiling, salted water for about 8 minutes, until translucent.
   Remove from water and drain.

– In a buttered 3-quart baking dish, alternate 3 to 4 layers of fennel, cheese, and
   prosciutto.

– Top with cubed butter and sprinkle with parmesan cheese. Season generously with
   salt and pepper.

– Bake for 20 to 25 minutes, until bubbly and nicely browned.

NOTE: Gratin can be refrigerated overnight, prior to baking, which makes it a great dish
for Thanksgiving. Bake the next day, as instructed.

FOOD SOURCES: Cookbook, Sprouts Farmers Market, farmers' markets for fennel;
Claro's Italian Markets and Roma Italian Deli and Grocery for prosciutto and Taleggio
and parmesan cheese.

ROASTED POTATOES WITH TARRAGON AND SHALLOT CRÈME FRAÎCHE

Crème Fraîche is the basis for so many final touches to simple dishes. One favorite way to extend its use is to add complementary flavors to its tart creaminess.

Serves 4 to 6

Preheat oven to 375°.

INGREDIENTS for Roasted Potatoes

8 to 12 medium Yukon gold or red potatoes (2 per person), washed, unpeeled
2 to 3 tablespoons extra-virgin olive oil
Kosher salt
Freshly ground pepper

METHOD

– Cut potatoes in half lengthwise and then again lengthwise into quarters to make spears. If potatoes are large, cut the spears into eighths.

– Place potatoes in a bowl, add oil, and mix thoroughly.

– Distribute potatoes on a parchment-covered half-sheet pan.

– Salt and pepper generously.

– Bake for 35 to 40 minutes, turning potatoes once about halfway through.

INGREDIENTS for Tarragon and Shallot Crème Fraîche

½ cup Crème Fraîche (see page 38)
1 teaspoon dried tarragon, crumbled
1 small shallot, very finely diced
1 to 2 teaspoons fresh lemon juice
Salt to taste, about ¾ teaspoon

METHOD

– In a small serving bowl, add all ingredients and stir gently until combined thoroughly.

– Serve with roasted potatoes.

TRY THIS: This sauce is excellent with roasted chicken or as a sandwich spread for sliced chicken, turkey, or steak.

FOOD SOURCES: Good-quality potatoes really do elevate this dish. There is a noticeable difference between farmers' market produce and that big bag you are tempted to buy at the supermarket. Though more expensive, the taste of Yukon gold, red, or fingerling potatoes freshly harvested transforms this dish into a gourmet delight. For the potatoes, shallots, and tarragon, try Cookbook or the Altadena, Atwater Village, Hollywood, or Pasadena Certified farmers' markets.

ROASTED WINTER SQUASH

Nothing tastes more comforting than roasted squash, and it can be the start of a number of delicious dishes. Plain, it is a great side dish. Or it can be used in place of carrots for a soup.

Serves 2 to 4, depending on size of squash

Preheat oven to 350°.

INGREDIENTS

1 butternut or acorn squash
2 tablespoons or more olive oil
¾ teaspoon kosher salt (a generous sprinkling)
A few gratings nutmeg

METHOD

– Cut squash in half; be very careful, as winter squash skin is tough. Use a large, sharp knife. I slice the top of the squash off so that I can balance the squash securely when I cut down.

– Clean out seeds and pith with a spoon and discard.

– Place squash halves on a parchment-lined half-sheet pan, cut-side up.

– Brush on the olive oil, sprinkle with salt, and add a few gratings of nutmeg.

– Bake until soft, at least 1 hour.

TRY THIS: Sprinkle with cayenne pepper or spread a spoonful of apricot jam, marmalade, or maple syrup mixed with ½ teaspoon ground cinnamon.

YAM AND WINTER SQUASH PURÉE WITH CARAMELIZED ONIONS

This is hands down the most universally loved and one of the simplest vegetable dishes I have ever made. The flavors of slowly caramelized onions, the sweetness and mellowness of winter squash and yams, and a hint of nutmeg are truly delicious. This dish wins additional points, as it is very, very good for you. It's great with turkey or any slow-cooked meat, such as brisket.

Serves 8 as a side dish

Preheat oven to 350°.

INGREDIENTS

3 to 4 tablespoons olive oil, divided
3 medium onions, medium dice
1 large piece banana squash or 2 medium butternut squashes, cut in half lengthwise, seeded
6 medium yams, unpeeled
2 teaspoons salt
Freshly ground pepper
Fresh nutmeg, grated

METHOD

– Heat 2 tablespoons olive oil in a large, heavy-bottomed sauté pan.

– Add onions and cook over medium heat until translucent.

– Turn heat to low and allow onions to caramelize slowly until dark golden and sweet tasting, 10 to 15 minutes.

– In the meantime, brush cut side of squash with about 1 tablespoon oil.

– Place on a half-sheet baking pan; bake for 30 minutes.

– Prick yams with a fork on all sides and add them to the baking pan.

– Continue baking until squash and yams are soft, about 30 to 40 more minutes. Remove from oven, let cool, then scoop out flesh.

– Add caramelized onions and flesh of yams and squash to a food processor. If you don't have room for the full batch, do this in two batches. Blend until very smooth.

– Add 2 teaspoons salt, 5 or so grindings of black pepper, and a few gratings of nutmeg Taste and add more salt and nutmeg if needed; take care not to overwhelm this delicate dish. Blend to incorporate.

– Coat a large gratin dish with remaining olive oil. Add the purée and smooth the top.

– Cover dish with foil and bake for at least 30 minutes, until heated through and a crust is beginning to form on the sides of the dish.

NOTE: Can be made ahead. Rather than baking, cover purée with plastic wrap and refrigerate up to 2 days. To bake, add 10 to 15 minutes to baking time.

FOOD SOURCES: The best-quality, freshest vegetables ensure flavor. Look for produce at Altadena, Atwater Village, Hollywood, Pasadena Certified, or another local farmers' market.

RICOTTA CORN CAKES WITH PEPPERONCINI SAUCE

These are a fabulous first course when we are all in the mood to indulge, usually for Sunday evening dinners when Eric is barbecuing ribs. Pie is nice for dessert. Then we take an eating break for a week (not really).

Serves 4 to 8

INGREDIENTS

½ cup (1 stick) unsalted butter, divided
8 scallions, white and light green part only, thinly sliced
2 cups fresh corn kernels (about 4 medium ears)
2 cups lowfat ricotta cheese (the only thing that is lowfat in this recipe)
8 large eggs, beaten with fork or whisk
⅔ cup all-purpose flour
⅔ cup yellow cornmeal
2 teaspoons kosher salt
¼ teaspoon white pepper
2 cups Crème Fraîche (see page 38)
8 to 10 pepperoncini, minced, plus about 1 tablespoon liquid from jar

METHOD

– Melt 6 tablespoons butter in a large skillet over medium heat. Add scallions and sauté until softened and slightly caramelized, about 8 minutes. Stir frequently.

– Add corn kernels and cook until warmed and golden. Set aside in a bowl to cool.

– Add ricotta to vegetable mixture and mix thoroughly.

– In a separate bowl, mix beaten eggs, flour, cornmeal, salt, and white pepper. Fold in ricotta mixture until thoroughly combined. Let batter sit for 20 minutes.

– Combine Crème Fraîche, pepperoncini, and liquid in a small bowl. Set aside.

– In a large nonstick skillet over medium heat, melt 2 tablespoons butter until foamy.

– Add 1 large tablespoon batter per corn cake to the skillet. You can fry about 4 corn cakes at a time. Fry over medium-low heat for about 3 minutes on each side, until corn cake is golden brown and no longer runny.

– Remove corn cakes from skillet and drain on paper towels. Keep corn warm in a 250° oven until all corn cakes are ready. Serve on a warm platter with pepperoncini sauce on the side.

NOTE: Pepperoncini are Italian peppers that are fairly easy to find, as they are used in Italian antipasto salads. They are preserved with vinegar, which takes on their flavor and heat.

TRY THIS: For a sweet accompaniment, serve with applesauce and sour cream in place of the pepperoncini sauce.

VEGETABLE TIAN

Tian is a French provincial word for an oval gratin dish, which shares its name with the food cooked in it.

Serves 8

Preheat oven to 350°.

INGREDIENTS

½ cup long-grain rice
¼ cup olive oil, divided
2 pounds small zucchini, unpeeled, cut into ¼-inch slices
Salt and freshly ground pepper
1 small onion, chopped
2 shallots, chopped
2 cloves garlic, chopped
3 eggs, beaten
¼ cup grated parmesan cheese, plus a bit more for the top
3 tablespoons chopped parsley or basil
Zucchini flowers, finely sliced (optional)

METHOD

– Grease a 3-quart gratin dish.

– Cook rice in 1 cup boiling, salted water until just tender, about 10 minutes.

– Let rice sit to dry out, about 30 minutes. (It can be made the day before, or use leftover white cooked rice.)

– Heat 2 tablespoons oil in a large frying pan; add zucchini and salt and pepper to taste. Cook over low heat, stirring often, for about 20 minutes, or until tender.

– Drain zucchini on paper towels, then chop coarsely and place in a large mixing bowl.

– In the same frying pan, heat another tablespoon oil over medium heat. Add onion, shallots, and garlic; cook until soft but not browned. Add the mixture to the zucchini. Mix in rice.

– Add eggs, cheese, parsley or basil, and salt and pepper to taste.

– Spoon mixture into a gratin dish. Sprinkle with remaining parmesan and zucchini flowers, if using. Bake for 15 minutes, until set.

– Raise oven temperature to 400° and bake for 10 more minutes, or until browned.

Serve from the dish—great for leftovers, too!

TRY THIS: A tian may be prepared with almost any vegetable. Some of my favorites are spinach, swiss chard, and asparagus. Vegetables may also be combined: spinach with thinly sliced winter squash, cauliflower with zucchini, patty pan squash with tomatoes.

FOOD SOURCES: Buying your vegetables in season at quality grocery stores such as Cookbook and La Mayordomia Market, or at farmers' markets is always recommended. The taste of freshness and quality comes through in this simple dish, where vegetables are the star.

Rumi, holding two of his favored kitchen tools: a glass of wine and a good knife.

RUMI MAHMOOD

"The world is his oyster" has a special culinary application for Rumi, a Bangladeshi native who experienced a number of cultures as a child and young teen, thanks to his father's career as a diplomat. After a short posting in Manila, where Rumi attended the American International School, his parents sent him to live with his older, college-bound brother in St. Louis to continue his high school education. Inspired by necessity, he figured out how to re-create the family's dishes. As a fearless, self-taught cook, he has since moved well beyond those first dishes in expertise and imagination, naming his mother's refined cooking, Jacques Pepin, and the requirements of Islamic dietary laws, or halal, as influences on his own cooking style and knowledge.

Rumi's broad cultural experience and discerning palate are evident in his proficient interpretation of Bengali dishes, which he fuses with East and Southeast Asian ingredients and flavors. After a day observing him in the kitchen, I came away with a year's worth of cooking wisdom. Perhaps because Rumi's profession is real estate development, he is particularly adept at breaking down a project into its component parts. And in his cooking, as in the building of a home, quality is assured through care and an attention to presentation. For all of us who did not have the opportunity to watch and learn about Indian and Bengali food traditions at the side of an accomplished mentor, a small portion of Rumi's kitchen wisdom follows.

Curries are multistep affairs, so do as much as you can on the front end: Parboil and cube potatoes or any slow-cooking vegetable; chop vegetables; prep meat; toast and grind spices. Patience is the first requirement to making a great base sauce for curries. Begin with onions and ginger in a generous amount of oil. Add spices and chiles. These should cook for quite some time, about 20 to 30 minutes, to mellow and mature the flavors; otherwise the base sauce can taste raw.

Add the garlic after the onions, ginger, and spices have been cooking a while, 15 minutes or so, to avoid burning the garlic. While the onions, ginger, and garlic are cooking, add a small amount of brown sugar for flavor and to caramelize the sauce. Add water at the end of the cooking cycle and very sparingly, or the sauce will taste raw and watered down. Keep a cup of water on the side and add a fifth or so at a time to loosen and moisten the sauce. When oil rises to the surface, the base sauce is done.

Fuss within reason, however; in some cases, ready-made or frozen is fine. Spinach is flash-frozen immediately after picking; Japanese food products, such as S&B curry powder are of very high quality; a bouillon cube—Rumi prefers Knorr for its superior quality—adds flavor as well as saltiness to a dish.

And what are his favorite foods? A good old American burger—crusty outside and juicy inside; French food for its ingredients, technique, and intense tradition; Baltimore crabs in any form, but especially crab cakes; New Orleans food; shrimp and grits; Japanese sushi for its celebration of incredible freshness and pure unadulterated flavors. Most of all, rice and "saucy" foods: "We all go back to our roots."

Paratha flatbread
Rumi's mother—his first taste influence—introduced him to light and refined cuisine. A favorite dish was a tangy potato curry served with paratha.

Pan de sal
Rumi's early teens were spent in Manila. Pan de sal rolls are a delicious Filipino treat.

A chicken from the Cartimar market in Manila
Rumi learned to butcher in adherence to halal precepts while living in the Philippines.

Crab cake
Rumi considers Baltimore crabs some of the best tasting. "A grocery-store crab cake in Baltimore is better than a five-star crab cake anywhere else."

Mortar and pestle
A favored tool; Rumi uses this almost daily to grind fresh spices.

Curry
In all of its variations, delicious proof of Rumi's proficiency as a cook.

The hamburger
Rumi and I are in complete agreement: crusty on the outside, juicy on the inside.

Jaques Pepin
Rumi's most admired chef and teacher, renowned for technique, quality, authenticity.

French food
Another of this omnivore's favored foods, for its precision and intense tradition.

Rice
Rice in all of its varieties, including kala jeera, named after the cumin seed for its shape and small size.

Seafood and Meat

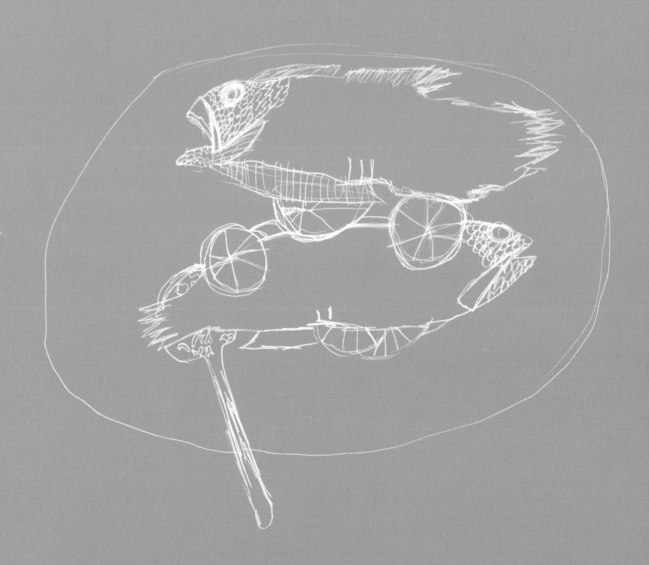

Garni Meat Market owner Alex Khachoyan and his son, Harut Khachoyan.

PÂTÉ MAISON in Memory of My Dad

Every Christmas, I made this pâté for my dad. It was his favorite present, which he shared grudgingly throughout the day. Even my stepmom, Margie, who normally found liver inedible, could tolerate this—and did.

Serves 4 to 6

INGREDIENTS

1 pound chicken livers
1 cup (2 sticks) unsalted butter, divided
½ cup finely chopped onion
1 small green apple, peeled and chopped
⅛ cup Drambuie or cognac
2 tablespoons cream, plus more if needed
1 teaspoon fresh lemon juice
1 teaspoon salt
Few grinds fresh pepper

METHOD

– Wash chicken livers, remove tendons, pat them dry, and cut them into large pieces.

– In a frying pan, melt ¼ cup butter and add the chopped onion. Cook over medium heat for 5 to 7 minutes, until the onions are soft.

– Add apple and cook 3 to 4 more minutes.

– When soft, transfer to a food processor fitted with a steel blade. (Leave a bit of the cooked butter in the pan.)

– Fry livers in the same pan over high heat. Cook and turn until they are browned but pink on the inside.

– Add Drambuie or cognac to the pan. Let the alcohol burn out. Add the liver, its drippings, and cream to the food processor and blend. Add a bit more cream if necessary.

– Dice ¾ cup butter. Add the butter, bit by bit, to the liver mixture and blend.

– Stir in lemon juice, salt, and a few grinds of pepper.

– Pack mixture in two small tureens or one large covered jar and refrigerate. Serve garnished with parsley.

NOTE: Crostini (see page 61) taste great with this pâté.

TRY THIS: Pour ¼ cup melted unsalted butter over the cooled pâté. Add a few grindings of pepper. Cool again. The butter makes for a much more attractive-looking dish and adds a bit more richness. Necessary? No. Delicious? Yes.

FOOD SOURCE: Whole Foods, as you want excellent-quality organic chicken livers. Just think about what this organ does.

MARIO'S QUESO FUNDIDO

My husband, Eric, and I first tasted this rich, beautiful dish at Mario Rodriguez's home. Eric is a dedicated sausage-maker and brought homemade chorizo. Monica, Mario's wife, made guacamole (see page 144) with avocados from their tree. These tastes lead me back to Mario again and again; his skill and imagination with all things edible remain an inspiration.

Serves 4

INGREDIENTS

½ tablespoon olive oil or lard
½ cup finely diced onion
8 ounces chorizo
Kosher salt to taste
1 pound asadero cheese (or Oaxaca or jack cheese as second choice), shredded

METHOD

– Heat a cast-iron or other heavy-bottomed, well-seasoned skillet over medium heat.

– Add oil or lard and heat.

– Add onion and sauté until soft.

– Remove chorizo from casing and add to skillet. As you sauté, break the chorizo down with a spoon until it begins to crumble. Continue to sauté until chorizo is browned, about 5 to 10 minutes. Add salt to taste.

– Add cheese to chorizo mixture and stir it in until it melts. Avoid heating the mixture too long after the cheese melts or the cheese will become tough.

– Serve immediately. (Mario uses the cast-iron skillet in which the queso fundido was cooked.)

– Optional garnishes include a couple pinches of chopped cilantro leaves or a tablespoon of pico de gallo tipped into the center. I used a few of Minh's Geranium Pickled Baby Onions (see page 51).

– Serve with corn tortillas or chips.

FOOD SOURCES: Find chorizo, cheese, and tortillas at Los Cinco Puntos, La Mayordomia Market, El Mercado de Los Angeles, Rincon Argentino, Super A Foods, Vallarta Supermarkets.

DOUG'S SALMON

Based on a recipe from the Steamboat Inn in Steamboat, Oregon. This is truly my favorite salmon recipe.

Serves 2 to 3

INGREDIENTS

3 tablespoons dried thyme or 4 to 5 tablespoons fresh thyme, finely chopped
¼ cup soy sauce
1 tablespoon olive oil
4 cloves garlic, pressed
2 tablespoons fresh lemon juice
1 pound filet of wild silver salmon or Chinook salmon

METHOD

– In a shallow ½-quart dish, mix thyme, soy sauce, olive oil, garlic, and lemon juice to create a marinade. Dip salmon skin-side first and turn over to flesh-side down. Marinate for 30 minutes.

– Heat grill to approximately 400°.

– Layer 2 sheets of aluminum foil together, and fold to form a low-sided pan. Place this on the grill. Put salmon on foil pan, skin-side down. Pour remaining marinade into the pan. Cook 20 minutes, being careful to not dry out the salmon. Check for doneness; the salmon should be flaky but still moist. Remove with a spatula. Carefully remove skin. Serve with rice and grilled vegetables.

FOOD SOURCES: Once again, I highly recommend shopping at a reputable fishmonger; Fish King is my go-to, always worth a special trip.

EASY MUSSELS

I learned about more "exotic" cooking ingredients from my friend Sylvie Poitrier Sobbotke, whom I met in Germany in the early 1980s. She was from the Strasbourg region of France, where food is simple but delicious. Sylvie served these to me as a treat shortly after my daughter, Nori, was born. I have never forgotten how delicious this dinner was.

4 servings

INGREDIENTS
3½ to 4 pounds mussels (¾ to 1 pound per person)
3 to 4 tablespoons unsalted butter
2 to 3 shallots, finely chopped
Pinch cayenne pepper
Pinch kosher salt
1 bottle good dry white wine
2 tablespoons flat-leaf parsley, chopped

METHOD
– Scrub mussels under cold water, discarding any that are open. They should be tightly shut. Keep cold until ready to cook; I hold them in an ice-water bath.

– Heat a large, heavy saucepan over medium heat, add butter, shallots, cayenne pepper, and salt.

– Cook over low heat until shallots are translucent.

– Add wine slowly and continue to cook until liquid is reduced a bit.

– Drain mussels and add to pan. Cover and continue cooking over low heat for a few minutes, until mussels are wide open. Discard any that do not open.

– Divide mussels into four large bowls. Pour broth over each serving and top with a large pinch of parsley.

– Accompany with toasted ciabatta or baguette with plenty of butter and a simple green salad with vinaigrette.

TRY THIS: As the shallots are cooking, add a link of crumbled chorizo, or ½ cup cubed, fried pancetta, or a thinly sliced link of lap cheong Chinese sausage. The broth is also very adaptable. Try adding Minh's favorite "Asian mirepoix": a generous slice of peeled ginger, 1 large shallot, peeled and cut in half, and 1 stalk lemongrass, peeled and cut in half.

FOOD SOURCES: Fish King for mussels; 168 Market and H Mart for Chinese sausage, ginger, shallot, lemongrass; La Mayordomia Market, Super A Foods, Vallarta Supermarkets for chorizo; Claro's Italian Markets, Roma Italian Deli and Grocery, Truffle Brothers for pancetta.

RUMI'S SHRIMP DOPIAZA

Dopiaza is Bengali for two onions; it is a delicious spicy, tomato-based curry. Rumi Mahmood suggests using a wok or deep skillet, as the size and shape are optimal for distributing heat. Do not hurry this dish; each step allows for the mellowing of flavors. Serve over medium- or long-grain rice.

Serves 8

INGREDIENTS

2½ pounds shrimp, large (26 to 30 count per pound) or jumbo (16 to 20 count per pound)

3 tablespoons peeled, finely chopped ginger, divided

2 rounded teaspoons turmeric, divided

4 cloves garlic, finely chopped (about 2 teaspoons)

2 jalapeño peppers, finely chopped, divided (seed peppers to moderate heat)

6 tablespoons vegetable oil, plus more for greasing the skillet

2 small onions, divided (1 coarsely chopped, the other sliced and then cut crosswise)

½ teaspoon sugar

2 teaspoons cayenne or red pepper flakes

2 rounded teaspoons paprika

2 medium tomatoes, coarsely chopped

1 teaspoon or more kosher salt, divided

½ cup chopped cilantro (stems and leaves)

METHOD

– Peel, devein, and rinse shrimp. Dry by laying shrimp on a half-sheet baking pan lined with a length of paper towel. Dab surface of shrimp with paper towel as well. In a medium bowl, thoroughly combine shrimp, 1 rounded tablespoon chopped ginger, 1 teaspoon turmeric, 1 teaspoon garlic, and 1 chopped jalapeño. Refrigerate shrimp until ready to use.

– In a wok or deep skillet, warm oil over medium heat. Sauté chopped onion until translucent. Add remaining ginger and garlic; continue cooking until garlic is translucent.

– Add sugar and cook until onion, ginger, and garlic turn golden-brown; reduce heat to low and add remaining jalapeño and turmeric. Add cayenne or red pepper flakes and paprika.

– Continue cooking for 10 to 15 minutes. Spices must be toasted sufficiently before adding water or curry will taste raw. If mixture begins to stick or burn, add water—no more than 1 tablespoon at a time. This is similar to deglazing a pan, but liquid is used throughout the cooking process and much more sparingly. Spread sauce out to heat evenly as you cook.

– Add tomato and continue to cook, "deglazing" as necessary. After about 10 minutes, tomato will be thoroughly incorporated into sauce. At this point, you should see the oil separating from the sauce. Add the sliced onion and cook for another 10 minutes, or until onions are barely softened, then add ¾ teaspoon salt. Taste, and add more salt if desired. Let sauce mellow over very low heat while you sauté the shrimp.

– Add a film of oil to a cast-iron or other heavy skillet and warm over medium-high heat. Add spiced shrimp and a large pinch of salt; sauté until shrimp is opaque on each side. Remove from heat immediately. Add shrimp to sauce. Serve with a pinch of cilantro per person.

TRY THIS: Rumi's recipe is a "dry curry." If you prefer more sauce, add ½ cup hot water. Or for a malai (cream) variation, add cilantro to the finished curry, along with ¾ can coconut milk or yogurt thinned with water to the consistency of milk for a total of 1 cup. Heat to a light boil and cook until cilantro is softened. For another variation, substitute 2½ pounds skinless, boneless chicken breasts, cut into cubes, for the shrimp. Sauté 15 to 20 minutes, until cooked through.

FOOD SOURCES: For shrimp, Fish King and H Mart; for spices, H Mart, India Food and Spices, Namaste Spiceland, Punjab Indian Grocery Store.

Rumi's Shrimp Dopiaza plated with Saag (see page 156).

SEAFOOD RISOTTO

Serves 2 as a main dish, 4 as a first course

INGREDIENTS

2 tablespoons butter, divided
1 shallot, minced
Kosher salt
1 cup arborio, carnaroli, or Koda Farms Heirloom Kokuho Rose rice
1 or so cups good white wine (drinking quality)
3 or so cups chicken broth (best is homemade, see pages 34 and 35)
Saffron threads (optional)
6 clams
½ pound bay scallops
½ pound large, raw shrimp, cleaned
Large pinch hot chili powder
Tiny pinch ghost pepper salt
Few grinds fresh pepper, coarse grind

METHOD

– In a large sauté pan (12-inch or larger) over medium heat, melt 1 tablespoon butter until foamy. Add shallot and cook until softened; add a bit of kosher salt to taste.

– Add rice and stir until coated with butter. Turn heat to medium-low. Add about ¼ cup wine and stir.

– In a large saucepan over medium heat, bring chicken broth to a simmer; reduce heat to maintain a low simmer.

– Add warmed chicken broth, ladleful by ladleful, to rice, waiting in between for rice to absorb the liquid. Alternating with the broth, add remaining wine in ¼ cup increments. Stir fairly constantly while adding broth and wine. Stop when rice is al dente: soft but not mushy, about 30 minutes. Be careful here because the seafood releases additional liquid as it cooks.

– Stir in saffron, if using, and remaining butter. The rice should be moist.

– Add clams, reduce heat, cover, and wait a few minutes for clams to begin to open. (Discard any that do not open.) Add scallops and shrimp; cover pan and cook another 3 to 5 minutes. Check occasionally to be sure you are not overcooking the seafood.

– Add chili powder, ghost pepper salt, and ground pepper; add more kosher salt if needed. Stir again and serve. Do not add parmesan cheese—a no-no with seafood in true Italian cooking.

TRY THIS: Use Minh's Habanero and Kumquat Salt (see page 51) for ghost pepper salt.

FOOD SOURCES: Fish King for seafood; Claro's Italian Markets, Cookbook, Koda Farms at Hollywood Farmers' Market, Roma Italian Deli and Grocery for rice.

"I don't think I've ever managed anything with this much nuance. The subtle kick provided by the ghost pepper salt and chili powder put it over the top."
ANNA GANAHL, *an intermediate cook eager to master basics and try new recipes*

ERIC'S ROASTED CHICKEN

Serves 4 to 8

Preheat oven to 375°.

INGREDIENTS

1 whole chicken (a smaller fryer serves 4 to 6; a roasting chicken serves 6 to 8)
2 teaspoons kosher salt

METHOD

– Cut away fat flaps from the opening of the chicken cavity. Rinse chicken inside and out; pat dry with a paper towel.

– Place salt in a small bowl. Liberally salt chicken inside and out.

– Place chicken on rack in shallow ovenproof pan, breast and legs facing up.

– Roast until chicken is done, 170° internal temperature, or until juices run clear when pierced with a fork, at least 1 hour.

– Remove chicken from oven, cover loosely with aluminum foil, and let rest for about 10 minutes. If joints are pink or red, chicken needs about 10 more minutes.

– Carve and serve. Great with Simple Pan Gravy (below), and Shirley Moore's Pilaf (see page 62), baked or new potatoes, or couscous.

NOTE: Raw chicken can be a breeding ground for salmonella. Do not use a wooden chopping board when cutting. Use surfaces that do not absorb liquid—your sink works well. Wash your hands in hot soapy water after you have touched the chicken. When seasoning, use a spoon.

TRY THIS: Place a halved lemon in chicken cavity. Combine 3 tablespoons minced fresh thyme, 1 tablespoon extra-virgin olive oil, and 1 tablespoon salt. Generously spread over surface of chicken skin. Or spread about ¼ cup (½ stick) unsalted, room-temperature butter over skin, then salt and pepper generously.

SIMPLE PAN GRAVY

Remove cooked chicken from roasting pan to a cutting board. Pour out fat from pan, taking care to leave the pan juices. The fat looks clear and slightly golden in color and rises to the top. You cannot remove all of it, nor do you want to. Place the roasting pan on the stove top; you will probably need two burners. Turn to low heat, add a generous knob of butter, and begin scraping the delicious roasted bits from bottom and sides of the pan. Add ½ to 1 cup white wine. Continue scraping. Remove about 1 tablespoon of the liquid and combine with about 1 teaspoon cornstarch. Return mixture to pan; continue stirring and scraping until contents thicken. Add ¼ to ½ cup cream or half-and-half, if desired. It is usually not necessary to add salt, as much of the seasoning remains in the pan juices. If your roasting pan is too large to pick up and pour out the fat easily, pour all of the juices into a fat separator as an interim step.

"For someone who has literally never roasted a chicken, it turned out perfectly, and I was as proud as I was amazed at myself!"
BETSY CLANCY, *novice cook and recipe tester*

CHICKEN TIKKA

Serves 4 to 6

Preheat oven to 400°.

INGREDIENTS

1½ cups Greek yogurt

2 cloves garlic, crushed

2 teaspoons crushed ginger root, grated or chopped very, very fine

2 teaspoons Sriracha Hot Chili Sauce

1½ tablespoons canola or vegetable oil

Fresh lemon juice (just a bit)

2 teaspoons salt

1 teaspoon Garam Masala (see below)

1 whole cut-up chicken; cut breast into 2 pieces each if chicken is large

METHOD

– In a large glass bowl, mix together first 8 ingredients (through Garam Marsala).

– Add chicken pieces; make sure all pieces are completely coated with yogurt mixture.

– Marinate in the refrigerator overnight, or 2 to 3 hours minimum.

– Place chicken pieces on a rack in a roasting pan.

– Roast until done (165° minimum), about 25 minutes, turning at least once.

– Serve with chutney, thinly sliced onions, and lemon wedges.

GARAM MASALA

Garam Masala is a roasted spice blend that is the basis for many Indian dishes.

INGREDIENTS

½ cup cumin seeds

2 tablespoons coriander seeds

4 cinnamon sticks, each 2 inches long

10 to 12 green or black shelled cardamom seeds, bruised

10 whole cloves

½ nutmeg, broken

1 tablespoon black peppercorns

5 bay leaves

METHOD

– Put all the spices in a dry pan (preferably nonstick) and heat over very low heat, shaking the pan from time to time, up to 10 minutes.

– When the spices give off a fragrance, remove from heat, allow to cool slightly, then grind finely in a coffee mill or electric blender.

– Store in an airtight jar. If stored in the freezer, spices keep indefinitely.

MAHOGANY CHICKEN

Our son, John, named this chicken because of its beautiful color. It remains one of his favorite dishes.

Serves 4 to 6

Preheat oven to 350°.

INGREDIENTS

1 whole chicken, roaster or fryer (2½ to 5 pounds)
1 cup soy sauce
1 cup canola or peanut oil
¼ cup sesame oil
4 tablespoons honey
Juice of 1 lemon
3 to 4 cloves garlic, pressed
Salt and freshly ground pepper

METHOD

– Place whole chicken in a large glass bowl.

– In a small bowl, combine all other ingredients and mix with a whisk. Pour mixture over chicken, turning chicken to moisten. Marinate in the refrigerator for at least 3 hours, turning chicken frequently.

– Remove chicken from marinade and place on a rack in a roasting pan.

– Baste chicken with marinade while it is roasting. The chicken will turn a deep mahogany color.

– Roast until chicken is done, 165° to 170° internal temperature, or until juices run clear when pierced with a fork, at least 1 hour.

– Remove from oven and let sit for about 10 minutes before carving.

TRY THIS: You can roast carrots along with the chicken: Coat peeled carrots with olive oil; begin roasting 15 to 20 minutes before adding chicken. This dish is a natural to serve with Fried Rice (see page 134) or Black Rice with Makrut Lime Leaves (see page 133).

Roasted Turkey Breast with Fennel served with Roasted Potatoes with Tarragon and Shallot Crème Fraîche (see page 158).

ROASTED TURKEY BREAST WITH FENNEL

Before I remarried, money was scarce, but that didn't stop my daughter, Nori, and me from enjoying our meals. One great way was to roast a turkey breast on Sunday and serve it with roasted potatoes, salad, etc. The breast lasted days, morphing into several great leftovers, such as turkey Waldorf salad, turkey enchiladas, turkey quesadillas, and lunch sandwiches.

Makes about 8 servings

Preheat oven to 450°.

INGREDIENTS
1 large bone-in turkey breast with skin (3 to 4 pounds)
1 stalk fennel, fronds only (you can save the bulb for Fennel Gratin [see page 157] or a salad)
3 to 5 cloves garlic, peeled and halved
Kosher salt
Freshly ground pepper

METHOD
– Wash turkey breast, drain, and pat dry. Rinse fennel fronds and pat dry.

– Slide your hand between turkey skin and breast and carefully tuck fennel between skin and meat.

– Cut ½-inch slits through turkey skin into the breast meat; push garlic cloves into each slit. Generously salt and pepper breast on all sides.

– Place breast skin-side up on a rack set into an ovenproof baking pan. Roast for 20 minutes, then turn the oven down to 350°. Roast turkey until juices run clear, about 1 more hour. Internal temperature should be 165° to 170° with an instant-read thermometer. Turkey will continue to cook after it is out of the oven, so do not let temperature go higher than 170° or it will dry out.

– Let turkey rest on a cutting board for about 15 minutes. Slice and serve.

NOTE: Safety instructions for chicken apply to turkey as well (see page 182).

RUMI'S JHAL GOSHT (BEEF OR LAMB CURRY)

I met Rumi Mahmood through chef and good friend Onil Chibás. Lucky me—both live only five minutes away! Serve this tasty dish with rice, naan bread, or paratha.

Serves 4

INGREDIENTS

3 tablespoons vegetable oil
1 large onion, coarsely chopped
Curry spices (see below)
1½ pounds lamb or beef stew meat
1 cup yogurt
1 tablespoon tomato paste
2 tablespoons chopped fresh cilantro (stems and leaves)

CURRY INGREDIENTS

1 to 2 teaspoons cayenne pepper or red pepper flakes (depending on heat tolerance)
1 jalapeño pepper, chopped (seed and devein pepper to moderate heat)
1 teaspoon ground coriander
1 teaspoon ground cumin
1 teaspoon ground turmeric
3 to 4 cloves garlic, finely chopped
2 teaspoons finely chopped ginger
1 teaspoon paprika
1 teaspoon each kosher salt and sugar
2 bay leaves
2 to 3 green or black cardamom pods, cracked open
1 cinnamon stick
4 whole cloves
½ teaspoon nutmeg (freshly grated is best)

METHOD

– Heat oil in a wok or deep skillet over medium heat; add onion and sauté until translucent to light brown. Add curry spices and stir well. Let spices cook, then add water sparingly to avoid sticking or burning—no more than 1 tablespoon at a time–throughout the cooking process, 6 to 8 minutes to develop flavor.

– Add meat, stirring well to distribute; cook over medium to high heat until well seared.

– Reduce heat to medium-low. Add yogurt, tomato paste, and cilantro.

– Cover and continue to braise for 40 to 50 minutes, until meat is tender.

– Remove cloves, bay leaves, cinnamon stick, and cardamom pods.

TRY THIS: Substitute 1 whole chicken cut into generous pieces; braise until golden brown, then cook for 30 minutes. Jhal Gosht tastes great with Rangpur lime marmalade (see page 75). It is a great filling for Turmeric Chili Crêpes (see page 57).

FOOD SOURCES: H Mart, India Food and Spices, Namaste Spiceland, Punjab Indian Grocery Store.

Rumi's Jhal Gosht Curry served with *dahl* (cooked lentils) and *raita* (yogurt with cucumber).

TRI-TIP ROAST

Here is another really easy great dish. It requires hardly any time and is so, so good. The leftovers make delicious sandwiches or an ingredient for composed salads for lunch the next day. Note: This is not a diet cut of meat. It is good because of the fat.

Serves 8 hungry folk

Preheat oven to 350°.

INGREDIENTS
2 to 3 pounds tri-tip roast
Salt and pepper

METHOD

– Salt and pepper roast liberally on both sides.

– Place roast fat-side up on a rack set in a roasting pan.

– Roast for 35 to 40 minutes, or until internal temperature is 145° for medium rare.

– Remove roast from oven and let rest for at least 10 minutes. Slice with fat on. Serve with horseradish or strong mustard.

NOTE: If you want to serve baked potatoes with your tri-tip, start baking them about 50 minutes prior to putting the roast in the oven.

TRY THIS: Here's an example of a great sandwich with tri-tip: Spread good bread— ciabatta or other hearty bread—with garlic butter or olive oil and toast in a toaster oven or under the broiler. Add thin slices of rare tri-tip, crumble blue cheese on top, and return to the toaster oven for a minute or two.

FOOD SOURCE: Armen Market, Garni Meat Market, Schreiner's Fine Sausages

"The tri-tip instructions were easy to follow, and the results were superb. My first attempt resulted in a delicious dinner that was followed by several luscious roast beef sandwiches over the next couple of days."
BETSY CLANCY, *novice cook, recipe tester*

SYLVIA'S ITALIAN MEATBALLS, The Best!

Another basic and satisfying recipe from Sylvia, my good friend Barbara's mother. Barbara's record of her mother's recipe contains no actual measurements, so she suggests starting with 1 teaspoon of each spice and adding more to your taste. You can fry a sample amount of the meat mixture to test for seasonings.

Serves 8

INGREDIENTS

2 pounds ground beef (or you can use ground turkey for lowfat meatballs)
1 egg
Salt and pepper
2 to 3 cloves garlic, crushed through a garlic press or finely minced
Dried oregano
½ cup breadcrumbs (Almost any kind works. Sylvia used plain breadcrumbs from a box. I often use up stale bread by drying it out for a day and making crumbs in the food processor.)
½ cup cold water
Francesca's Tomato Sauce (double recipe, see page 125) or 1 quart good-quality jarred tomato sauce

METHOD

– In a large bowl, mix together all ingredients except for tomato sauce. Shape into 2-inch balls.

– Pour tomato sauce into a large, deep saucepan, add meatballs, and simmer over low heat for 30 minutes, or until cooked through.

– Serve over cooked pasta or in toasted split rolls with some sauce for meatball sandwiches.

TRY THIS: Like the ubiquitous noodle, meatballs offer tremendous license to experiment. Sylvia often browned her meatballs on the outside and finished cooking as above. This creates a crusty texture. One of my favorite variations is to add 2 teaspoons Vietnamese fish sauce or 2 finely chopped anchovy filets to the ground meat mixture as a more luscious alternative to salt. I coat the meatballs in panko prior to browning them. If you wish to use the meatballs without tomato sauce, continue cooking on low heat for about 10 minutes beyond browning. They are delicious with sautéed swiss chard, broccoli rabe, or spinach, accompanied by a simple pasta of olive oil, garlic, and parmesan.

FOOD SOURCE: Garni Meat Market (Alex, the owner, will grind meat to your specifications), Schreiner's Fine Sausages.

FABULOUS SLOW-ROASTED PORK

Perfect for a dinner party, as this delicious dish practically cooks itself once it is in the oven.

Serves 8

Preheat oven to 450°.

INGREDIENTS

10 cloves garlic, peeled
½ cup fennel seeds
2 tablespoons coarse sea salt
½ teaspoon freshly ground pepper
5 to 6 small dried red chiles, crumbled, with seeds
1 boneless pork shoulder butt (6 to 7 pounds)
4 tablespoons olive oil, divided
Juice of 1 lemon
½ cup chicken broth

METHOD

– Using a mortar and pestle, crush garlic and fennel seeds and place in a small bowl. Add sea salt, pepper, and chiles and stir to combine.

– Cut 1-inch slits all over the surface of the pork, including the top and bottom of the meat. Push garlic mixture into the slits.

– Heat 2 tablespoons oil in a large, heavy Dutch oven over medium to low heat. Sear meat on all sides for 10 to 12 minutes per side. Do not allow garlic to burn. Remove roast from pot.

– Add ½ cup hot water to pan, stirring and scraping the bottom to deglaze.

– Return meat to pan, fatty-side up, and roast in the oven, uncovered, for 30 minutes.

– Pour lemon juice and broth over meat. Brush with the remaining oil.

– Reduce heat to 275°. Cover pan and roast meat for 6 to 8 hours, basting occasionally with pan juices.

– Roast will be done when meat falls apart when barely touched with a fork (check at about 6 hours; you don't want to dry out the meat).

– Remove roast from pot and place on a serving platter.

– Skim fat from pan drippings. Serve drippings on the side. Or make our friend Tony Silver's wonderful sauce: After skimming off fat, add some chicken broth, Drambuie, oregano, and a little bit of white wine. Cook for about 15 minutes. In a small bowl, mix a small amount of liquid from the pan with 1 tablespoon cornstarch (to avoid lumps), then stir into the sauce. Add a small amount of butter. Cook for about 10 minutes, until the flavors in the sauce come together and it no longer tastes of cornstarch.

TRY THIS: Great with Italian broccoli or collard greens. The leftover pork makes a great soft-taco filling.

FOOD SOURCES: Armen Market, La Princesita Carnicera y Tortilleria, Schreiner's Fine Sausages, Sprouts Farmers Market, Super A Foods, Vallarta Supermarkets.

CARNE ADOVADA

Based on a recipe from the Santa Fe School of Cooking.

Serves 8

INGREDIENTS

1/3 cup grapeseed oil
4 pounds pork loin or pork butt, cut into 3/4-inch cubes
2½ cups finely diced onion
2½ tablespoons minced garlic
4 cups chicken broth, divided
3 teaspoons ground coriander seed
2½ teaspoons dried Mexican oregano
2 teaspoons red chile flakes
¾ cup ground New Mexico red chile (medium heat)
3 tablespoons good-quality honey
3 tablespoons sherry vinegar
Salt to taste

METHOD

– Heat oil in a large skillet, then brown pork in small batches, pouring off most of the fat. Set pork aside. Add onions to pan and sauté until golden. Add garlic and cook for 1 minute.

– Deglaze with 1 cup chicken broth, loosening browned bits with a spoon.

– Place coriander, oregano, chile flakes, chili powder, and honey in the bowl of a food processor. Add onions, garlic, sherry vinegar, broth from the skillet, and 2 more cups chicken broth. Process until mixture is thoroughly combined.

– Place browned pork, chile marinade, and remaining 1 cup chicken broth in a heat-proof casserole.

– Stir to combine well: Cook 1 hour, uncovered, on low heat, or until meat is tender.

TRY THIS: Substitute goat for the pork.

FOOD SOURCES: Schreiner's Fine Sausages carries a full range of pork cuts. Goat and chiles may be purchased at La Princesita Carnicera y Tortilleria, Super A Foods, and Vallarta Supermarkets.

Sumi Chang *(left)* and Masako Yatabe Thomsen have been baking together for more than ten years. Masako, who trained as an architect, asked Sumi to mentor her, just as Nancy Silverton had mentored Sumi many years earlier.

SUMI CHANG

Like so many of her colleagues in the culinary world, Sumi did not set out to be one of our community's great pastry chefs. Guided by confidence and deep curiosity, she took a surprising fork in her life's road when she left her high-paying profession as an ICU nurse to become a minimum wage-earning prep cook at a high-end hotel restaurant. After an inspiring three-month baking course at Tante Marie's Cooking School in San Francisco, Sumi was hooked. She had no plan, but she knew that an internal shift had occurred in her identity—from hobbyist to serious baker—and she never looked back. Sumi describes baking as being in her DNA. Clearly it is, as the role of nurture in the nature/nurture equation was of little impact. She grew up in South Korea, where the idea of dessert is often a stick of chewing gum or a piece of fruit to moderate the spicy, fermented flavors of that country's cuisine.

Her journey to mastery is a case study in persistence, inner fortitude, single-mindedness, wonder, and patience. She showed up more than once during the early days of Nancy Silverton's La Brea Bakery in Los Angeles, hoping to work there. "I applied for a job at the bakery, but Nancy told me she didn't have any openings. I felt I needed to improve my résumé, so I came back after a year at the hotel, but they said no again; they didn't have any openings. So I said I really wanted to volunteer. I worked five days at the hotel and gave two days to the bakery." Within two weeks, she was hired and began a five-year tenure that ended as breakfast chef at Silverton's Campanile restaurant. She then applied her knowledge, skill, and confidence to open Europane Bakery in Pasadena more than twenty years ago.

Europane and Sumi became one and the same: welcoming, gracious, and deeply personal. And like the product of many artists, both the exquisite quality of her food and the community she created seem to appear without effort. While the actual reality of a baker's life is a rigorous work schedule beginning when most of us are sleeping, Sumi found her deepest reserves of energy and creativity during this quietest of times, sometimes as early as two o'clock in the morning, when she focused only on the qualities of her art: taste, flavor, and texture. "I would lose track of time."

Sumi sold Europane in 2017 after securing a buyer with sufficient business expertise to assure ongoing positions for her beloved employees. She is now planning a new venture: cooking instruction for small groups, co-taught with her baking partner of ten years, Masako Yatabe Thomsen, whom Sumi describes as "my left brain with an intelligent and perceptive palate."

Her next stage is bound to be another lesson in mastery, as she continues along an inspiring and authentic road without any predictable stopping point.

SUMI CHANG'S FOOD INFLUENCES

Fresh fruits
Fruit is a key ingredient for many of Sumi's baked goods.

Palmiers
Sumi loves baking French patisserie.

Tante Marie
Former cooking school in San Francisco, home of Sumi's first baking class.

Lemon Bar
Sumi's version is one of her many beloved signature desserts.

Offset spatula
Sumi's favorite tool.

Masako Yatabe Thomsen
Sumi's baking partner for ten years, described as "my left brain."

The Flavor Thesaurus
Guide to how flavors affect one another; one source for Sumi's creativity.

Map of France
Whenever possible, Sumi travels to France to refresh her baking technique.

Bread
One of the early adopters of artisanal bread-baking.

Nancy Silverton
Brilliant chef and restaurateur; the mentor who gave Sumi her first chance to demonstrate her baking talents.

Calendar
Sumi's most creative time is at two o'clock in the morning, when she is alone with her ideas.

Desserts—Yay!

Aladdin Nuthouse owner Gary Karalekian. With its inspiring variety of nuts and seeds, this store is often my first stop for making desserts.

PEGGY'S PAVLOVA

My dear friend Peggy began traveling early, as she was a diplomat's daughter. While in New Zealand, she tasted this exquisite dessert. It is delicious.

Serves 8

Preheat oven to 300°.

INGREDIENTS

4 egg whites, room temperature
Pinch cream of tartar (optional)
Pinch salt
½ cup granulated sugar
1½ teaspoons vanilla extract, divided
1 teaspoon white vinegar
1 tablespoon cornstarch
½ cup and 2 teaspoons superfine sugar
2 cups whipped cream (see note below)
½ cup fresh raspberries or blueberries
3 tablespoons Plum or Strawberry Jam (optional, see pages 70, 71, and 72)

METHOD

– Line a half-sheet pan with parchment paper.

– In a large bowl, beat egg whites with cream of tartar and salt until stiff peaks form.

– Gradually add granulated sugar, 1 tablespoon at a time, while continuing to beat.

– When all the sugar has been incorporated, add 1 teaspoon vanilla, vinegar, and cornstarch.

– Beat until very stiff, then fold in superfine sugar.

– Shape into a circle on the prepared pan. Use back of spoon to create peaks.

– Bake 10 minutes at 300°; turn oven down to 200°, and bake 1 hour and 20 minutes.

– Turn oven off and let pavlova cool for 30 minutes in the oven.

– To serve, spread pavlova with whipped cream and fresh berries. I add small dollops of homemade plum or strawberry jam for additional flavor.

NOTE: To whip cream, it helps to refrigerate your beaters and bowl. Pour whipping cream into a medium bowl. Using a hand mixer, beat on high until stiff peaks form. Add 2 teaspoons fine sugar and ½ teaspoon vanilla.

FOOD SOURCES: Great eggs do make a difference. Try Cookbook, Culture Club 101, or the Altadena, Atwater Village, Hollywood, or Pasadena Certified farmers' markets. Cookbook and Sprouts Farmers Market carry excellent dairy products.

CHRISTIANA'S BEET CHOCOLATE CAKE

My friend Christiana—an all-around lovely and talented human being—wrote a great food blog, *The Harmonious Kitchen,* that included this recipe. We LOVE this cake! It is moist and rich without being overly sweet. And beet haters are none the wiser.

Serves 14

Preheat oven to 350°.

INGREDIENTS for Cake

1½ cups flour, plus more for coating pans

4 ounces unsweetened chocolate

1 cup vegetable oil, divided

3 eggs

1½ cups sugar

2 cups puréed roasted or boiled beets (about 6 medium fresh beets); cook and purée beets the night before. Or use two 8-ounce packages Trader Joe's steamed baby beets and purée

1 tablespoon vanilla extract

2 teaspoons baking soda

¼ teaspoon salt

METHOD

- Prepare two 9-inch cake pans with oil and flour (see note below).

- Melt chocolate and ¼ cup oil in a double boiler; set aside to cool.

- Combine eggs and sugar in a large bowl and beat in remaining ¾ cup oil, chocolate mixture, puréed beets, and vanilla.

- Sift flour, baking soda, and salt into another large bowl. Stir the dry ingredients slowly into the wet ingredients, until the flour is just mixed.

- Pour batter into the prepared pans. It will be very "liquidy."

- Bake until a toothpick inserted comes out clean, 25 to 35 minutes. Check at 25 minutes; you may need to bake 5 or more additional minutes.

INGREDIENTS for Frosting

8 ounces cream cheese, softened

4 tablespoons (½ stick) butter, softened

2 cups powdered sugar

1 teaspoon vanilla extract

Zest from 1 orange

Candied Orange Peel (see page 78), optional

FOOD SOURCES: For eggs and cream cheese, Cookbook, Culture Club 101. For the chocolate, Janes Cake and Chocolate Supply and Surfas Culinary District.

METHOD

– In a large bowl, beat together cream cheese and butter with an electric mixer.

– With the mixer on low speed, add powdered sugar 1 cup at a time, until mixture is smooth and creamy. Beat in vanilla extract and orange zest.

– When cake is completely cooled, frost top of each cake layer with an offset spatula or butter knife, using about ⅓ of the frosting on the bottom layer and ⅔ for the top. If you are new to cake frosting, there are many online descriptions.

– Add thinly sliced candied orange peel, if using.

NOTE: To prepare pans, lightly brush oil on all inside surfaces of each pan. Sprinkle flour on each surface and swirl until pans are completely coated. I cut two rounds of parchment to line the bottom of each pan, to be sure the cake won't stick.

"Delicious! Not too sweet, just as described, but rich and moist."
DAVID SPIRO, *experienced baker, recipe tester*

GERMAN CHEESECAKE

Serves 16

Preheat oven to 350°.

INGREDIENTS for Crust

9 graham crackers (1 package)
1 teaspoon sugar
½ cup blanched, chopped almonds, toasted in a 350° oven for 10 to 15 minutes
4 tablespoons (½ stick) butter, melted, plus more for greasing pan

METHOD

– In a food processer, blend graham crackers until coarsely ground. Add sugar, almonds, and 4 tablespoons butter; mix until blended.

– Cut a round of parchment paper and place on the bottom of a 9-inch springform pan. Brush pan sides with melted butter.

– Press graham-cracker crust mixture into bottom and ½ inch up the sides of the pan.

– Bake for 10 minutes. Remove from oven and allow crust to cool.

INGREDIENTS for Filling

3 extra-large eggs, separated
⅓ cup vegetable or safflower oil
1 whole vanilla bean, split open, and ½ teaspoon vanilla extract, or 1½ teaspoons vanilla extract
Zest of 1 large lemon
8 ounces quark (if unavailable, use mascarpone)
2 cups plain whole-milk Greek-style yogurt
1 cup sugar
2 tablespoons cornstarch

METHOD

– Separate eggs, placing yolks in a small bowl and whites in a medium bowl.

– Add oil to yolks; mix thoroughly. Add the scratched-out interior of the vanilla bean, the vanilla extract, and lemon zest to oil and egg yolk mixture and set aside.

– Using a hand mixer, beat egg whites until stiff. Set aside.

– In a large bowl, beat quark; blend in yogurt, then mix in sugar until smooth. Combine with the egg yolk mixture. I use a hand mixer.

– Remove a large spoonful of batter to a small bowl and blend in the cornstarch. Add cornstarch mixture to batter and mix until evenly distributed.

– Fold in egg whites until just combined.

– Pour filling into crust. Bake on the second rack from the bottom for 60 minutes. Keep oven door closed. Turn off oven. Let cake cool in the oven for 2 hours. The cake will rise, become resistant to the touch, and then fall a bit as it cools. Refrigerate for 3 hours.

FOOD SOURCES: Schreiner's Fine Sausages sells a variety of German foods, including quark cheese. Call ahead to check availability.

POLENTA ALMOND CAKE

The texture of this dessert sits somewhere between cake and cornbread. Make sure to beat the sugar and butter sufficiently. Your patience and care will be rewarded by a delicious, very light cake.

Serves 8 to 10

Preheat oven to 350°.

INGREDIENTS

½ cup sliced almonds
½ cup whole almonds
½ cup finely ground polenta flour (*farina per polenta*)
½ cup unbleached flour
1½ tablespoons cornstarch
1 teaspoon baking powder
1 teaspoon salt
¾ cup (1½ sticks) unsalted butter, room temperature, plus 2 tablespoons melted
1¼ cup sugar, divided
3 large eggs
Zest of 1 orange, plus 3 tablespoons freshly squeezed orange juice
½ teaspoon vanilla extract

METHOD

– Spread sliced almonds on a half-sheet pan lined with parchment and bake until golden brown and fragrant, about 10 minutes. Set aside to cool.

– Place whole almonds in the bowl of a food processor fitted with a metal blade and process until finely ground. Transfer to a medium bowl; whisk in polenta, flour, cornstarch, baking powder, and salt. Set aside.

– In the bowl of a stand mixer fitted with a whisk attachment, cream butter and 1 cup sugar until the color and texture of whipped cream, about 20 to 30 minutes. Add eggs, one at a time, mixing after each addition. Continue beating 10 more minutes.

– Add orange zest, orange juice, and vanilla.

– With a rubber spatula gently fold dry ingredients into egg mixture.

– Spread melted butter on the bottom and sides of a 9-inch springform pan. Pour batter into prepared pan. Smooth top.

– Bake 30 to 35 minutes, until cake tester comes out clean. Do not overbake, or the cake will be very dry. Transfer pan to a wire rack to cool; then invert cake onto another wire rack and reinvert cake onto a serving plate.

– Heat 4 tablespoons sugar in a small frying pan until caramelized, about 5 minutes. Pour caramelized sugar over cake's surface and spread with a silicon basting brush.

– Top with toasted almonds while sugar is still syrupy. Avoid burning your fingers.

– Let cool completely before serving.

TRY THIS: Delicious with whipped cream or with Crème Fraîche (see page 38) and Citrus Marmalade (see page 75).

SYLVIA AND BARBARA'S CHOCOLATE ORANGE MARBLE CAKE

This recipe is more than fifty years old; it was developed by Sylvia and refined by her daughter, Barbara. It is a gorgeous cake in taste and looks. Serve with whipped cream.

Serves 10 to 12

Preheat oven to 350°.

INGREDIENTS

2¼ cups flour
2½ teaspoons baking powder
1 teaspoon salt
2 ounces unsweetened baking chocolate
¼ teaspoon baking soda
1 cup plus 1 tablespoon whole milk
⅔ cup unsalted butter, softened
1½ cups sugar
3 eggs
1 teaspoon vanilla extract
1 teaspoon orange extract
1½ tablespoons orange zest (from 1 large orange)

METHOD

– Grease a 6-cup nonstick Bundt pan.

– Sift flour, baking powder, and salt into a bowl.

– Melt chocolate in a small pan, or microwave in a small bowl for about 1 minute.

– Add baking soda and 1 tablespoon milk to chocolate. Chocolate will change texture and appear dry; when combined with the batter, it will smooth out. Set aside to cool.

– In a stand mixer using a flat beater, cream together butter and sugar until fluffy.

– Add eggs, one at a time, to butter and sugar mixture. Blend thoroughly.

– Add vanilla to remaining cup of milk.

– Add dry ingredients (flour, baking powder, and salt) and wet ingredients (vanilla and milk) to egg mixture, alternating between dry and wet, about ½ cup at a time, beginning and ending with dry.

– Divide batter into 2 parts, leaving half of the batter in the stand-mixer bowl and transferring the other half to a medium bowl.

– Add chocolate mixture to batter in the stand mixer and beat at least 3 minutes to incorporate thoroughly. The chocolate mixture will soften and combine easily into the batter, which should be smooth.

– To the other bowl, add orange extract and zest, and blend.

– Drop chocolate and orange batters alternately by large spoonfuls into prepared pan.

– Use a sharp knife to swirl the batters in a circular motion, being careful not to over-blend them. Use an offset spatula or butter knife to smooth the cake's surface.

– Bake 40 to 45 minutes, until a toothpick inserted into cake's center comes out clean.

– Cool completely on a wire rack before inverting. Wait another hour before serving.

BARBARA'S WHIPPED CREAM POUND CAKE

Barbara, my good friend since childhood, bakes this amazing cake anytime there is a special occasion. Fortunately, my visits always qualify! This cake has body, a subtle flavor, and incredible lightness, along with a crisp, sugary surface. While simple, the recipe requires paying attention to a few critical steps.

Serves 8 to 10

Preheat oven to 350°.

INGREDIENTS

Scant amount unsalted butter, to prepare the pan
3 cups and 2 tablespoons sugar, divided
3 cups flour
4 teaspoons baking powder
½ teaspoon kosher salt
2 cups whipping cream
4 eggs, room temperature, beaten
1 teaspoon almond extract (use pure almond extract; no substitutes)
¼ cup powdered sugar, or less

METHOD

– Butter a 6-cup Bundt pan, then add 2 tablespoons sugar to pan and rotate so the sugar coats the sides. Best to do this over the sink. Pour out excess sugar.

– In a medium bowl, sift flour with baking powder and salt. Set bowl aside.

– In a stand mixer using the whisk attachment, or in a bowl using an electric handheld mixer, beat whipping cream until thickened but still soft enough to flow slowly from the whisk. Be careful not to overbeat. When the cream begins to thicken, stop the mixer and test the cream. It should fall off the beaters but hold some of its shape when it drops back into the bowl. The handheld mixer will require longer beating time, as it is not as powerful.

– If using a stand mixer, exchange the whisk for the flat beater. With the mixer on, add sugar slowly, then eggs, and finally the almond extract. Continue beating on low for 3 additional minutes.

– Carefully add dry ingredients until just incorporated; do not overmix. Stop once to scrape the sides and bottom of bowl to incorporate any unmixed flour or cream.

– Turn into prepared pan. This is a batter that needs to be treated delicately. No rapping to even the surface. Just use an offset spatula, if necessary, to smooth the top.

– Bake in the upper-middle rack of your oven, 55 to 60 minutes, until a wooden skewer comes out clean. Remove immediately to a rack and cool completely before removing cake from pan. Sift a dusting of powdered sugar over the cake's surface and serve.

TRY THIS: Delicious as is, served with whipped cream and berries, or cut in layers and spread with lemon curd or with Citrus Marmalade (see page 75) and whipped cream.

A GREAT FLAN

This flan is light and does not have the cloying taste of flans made with condensed milk. Even the die-hard flan dislikers have given into this. It is low calorie, delicious, and a great dessert to serve after a heavy meal. Prepare flan the night before you plan to serve it, as it takes a while to firm up.

Serves 8

Preheat oven to 350°.

INGREDIENTS

4 whole cloves

2 whole allspice

4 cardamom pods, cracked open so seeds are showing

1 cinnamon stick, broken in 2 pieces

2 cups milk (whole milk is richer; lowfat is lower in calories; guess which one we like best?)

¾ cup plus 6 tablespoons sugar, divided

6 eggs

METHOD

– Combine cloves, allspice, cardamom pods, cinnamon stick, and milk in a 2-quart saucepan. Heat until milk smells fragrant and is hot but not boiling, about 5 minutes.

– Pour milk through a sieve into a small bowl to remove spices. Set aside to cool.

– In a nonstick frying pan over medium heat, melt ¾ cup sugar. Shake and tilt the pan, rather than stirring. When melted, the sugar will caramelize (watch for a golden brown color).

– Immediately pour syrup into a 9 x 2-inch deep round ceramic dish. Tilt pan quickly so syrup flows over bottom and slightly up sides.

– In a small bowl, beat together eggs and 6 tablespoons sugar.

– Gradually add the egg and sugar mixture to the cooled spice-flavored milk, stirring quickly with a whisk.

– Set caramel-lined pan in a larger ovenproof pan and pour egg mixture over the caramel.

– Add enough boiling water to the larger pan to come just halfway up the outside of the smaller pan.

– Bake for about 30 minutes, or until a deep crevice forms when center of custard is gently pushed with the back of a spoon; remove from oven.

– Carefully remove flan pan from hot water; refrigerate immediately. Chill at least 6 hours or overnight.

– When flan is set, run a butter knife around the inside of the pan to loosen. Place a large plate with a lip that more than covers the flan pan. Flip over quickly. The flan will release. There should be a great deal of lovely caramel syrup. Serve with whipped cream.

SUMI'S LEMON BARS FOR A CROWD

Lemon bars are part of Pasadena's event scene; there are few fundraisers or luncheons that don't conclude with these delicious, tart squares. Sumi Chang's are some of the best I have tasted, with a super lemony filling and buttery, flaky crust. Sumi writes, "Before you make anything, read the recipe and gather equipment and ingredients. I make it a practice to go over ingredients twice before starting to bake." This recipe can be cut in half for a smaller group.

Makes 24 bars

INGREDIENTS for Shortbread Crust

4 cups flour
1½ cups powdered sugar, sifted
1 pound (4 sticks) unsalted butter, chilled, cut into ½-inch cubes, plus more for greasing pan
½ teaspoon salt

METHOD

– In the bowl of a stand mixer fitted with the paddle attachment, or in a large bowl using a pastry cutter, cut in all ingredients until they come together to form a dough.

– Press dough along the bottom and up the sides of a buttered half-sheet baking pan. Use parchment on the bottom of the pan if you prefer, but butter the sides.

– Preheat oven to 350°.

– Set pan in the refrigerator for 30 minutes to let dough rest.

– Place pan in oven and bake until the crust is golden brown, about 30 minutes. Reduce oven temperature to 300°. Let crust cool while you make the filling.

INGREDIENTS for Lemon Filling

12 large eggs
5½ cups sugar
3 to 4 tablespoons lemon zest and 2 cups fresh lemon juice (8 to 10 medium lemons)
2 cups all-purpose flour
Powdered sugar for dusting

METHOD AND ASSEMBLY

– In a large bowl, thoroughly whisk together eggs, sugar, zest, lemon juice, and flour.

– Place baking sheet with prepared crust on a rack in the center of the oven.

– Carefully pour lemon filling into the crust.

– Bake at 300° for 35 to 40 minutes, until filling is set. It should not jiggle in the middle when you move the pan. Or test with a toothpick inserted in the middle; it should come out clean.

– Cool at room temperature, then dust with powdered sugar. Cut into 24 squares in the pan; remove from pan square by square.

– Sumi repurposes any extra dough as shortbread cookie dough.

POLVORONES (MEXICAN WEDDING COOKIES)

Inspired by Tomasa Mendoza, who made cookies similar to these for every happy occasion, including our wedding.

Makes about 4 dozen cookies

Preheat oven to 350°.

INGREDIENTS

¼ cup olive oil
Large sprig fresh rosemary
1 cup freshly ground walnuts (hand chop them with a knife to avoid grinding them
   too finely)
2 to 2½ cups sifted flour (depending on how round you want your cookies)
Pinch salt
1 cup (2 sticks) unsalted butter, softened
2 cups powdered sugar, divided

METHOD

– Heat oil and rosemary in a small saucepan over low heat until you can smell the rosemary; or heat oil and rosemary in a heat-proof cup in the microwave for 1 minute, or until fragrant. Remove rosemary.

– Combine ground walnuts, flour, and salt in a medium bowl. Mix in softened butter, little by little. Add 1 cup powdered sugar and mix well.

– Add rosemary-infused oil, bit by bit, just until dough holds together.

– Form dough into ¾-inch balls and place on parchment-lined half-sheet pan.

– Bake for 15 to 20 minutes, until just beginning to turn golden.

– Cool cookies completely on wire racks.

– Roll each cookie in powdered sugar. Store cookies in a tightly covered container for up to 5 days.

NOTE: These cookies seem simple, but they can be a bit tricky. If the dough is too wet, the cookies will not have the characteristic lightness that makes them so good. Add a bit of flour, but go easy. Do not attempt to roll cookies in the powdered sugar until they are completely cool. Otherwise, the cookies will turn into a gloppy mess.

FOOD SOURCES: Aladdin Nuthouse for the highest-quality, freshest nuts; also Sprouts Farmers Market, and farmers' markets throughout the region.

AUNT MINI'S BUTTER COOKIES

These cookies are beautiful: light, soft on the inside, crispy around the edges. They are the quintessential old-world cookie, with the scent of almonds and the bite of chocolate. They came to me after years of nagging my oldest and dearest friend, Barbara, for the recipe. Barbara writes, "Aunt Mini was a wonderful Jewish cook. Her table was overflowing with rich and delicious food. These cookies were my childhood favorite. She always had them ready for us when we took the ferry to her home on Staten Island for a Sunday dinner. She often snuck me one before dinner. This recipe is courtesy of my cousin Eileen, Mini's daughter."

Makes 50 to 60 cookies

INGREDIENTS

1¾ cups flour, plus more for dusting
½ teaspoon baking powder
½ teaspoon salt
1 cup (2 sticks) unsalted butter
1½ cups sugar, divided
3 eggs
1 teaspoon almond extract
12 ounces semisweet mini chocolate chips
1 tablespoon ground cinnamon

METHOD

– In a medium bowl, combine 1¾ cups flour, baking powder, and salt; set aside.

– In a large bowl, cream butter and 1¼ cups sugar.

– Add eggs, one at a time, to butter and sugar mixture, beating after each addition.

– Blend in almond extract.

– Slowly add dry ingredients, stirring until just blended.

– Fold in chocolate chips.

– Refrigerate, covered, overnight. You want this batter to be very cold before you bake.

– When you are ready to bake, preheat the oven to 350°.

– Mix remaining sugar and cinnamon in a small bowl; set aside.

– Place a small amount of flour in another small bowl. Form about 1 tablespoon of dough into a ball and roll in flour. Repeat, placing each ball 2 inches apart on a buttered or parchment-lined half-sheet pan. (Refrigerate remaining batter while each batch bakes.) Flatten each ball, pressing down gently with your palm or fingers.

– Sprinkle each cookie generously with cinnamon sugar.

– Bake 12 to 15 minutes, or until edges turn golden brown. Let cool on a rack.

NOTE: These cookies freeze very well for up to 2 months. You can double the recipe for a crowd.

FOOD SOURCES: Jane's Cake and Chocolate Supply, Nicole's Market & Café, Surfas Culinary District.

CRISPY PEANUT BUTTER COOKIES

These are husband Eric's favorites. There is nothing subtle here—rather, they are bold, salty, sweet little bombs.

Makes about 5 dozen cookies

Preheat oven to 350°.

INGREDIENTS

2½ cups unbleached all-purpose flour
½ teaspoon baking soda
½ teaspoon baking powder
1 teaspoon salt
1 cup (2 sticks) unsalted butter, softened but still cool
1½ cups sugar
½ cup light brown sugar, packed
1 cup peanut butter, extra-crunchy
2 large eggs
2 teaspoons vanilla extract
1 tablespoon dark molasses
1 cup salted dry-roasted peanuts, ground in a food processor to resemble breadcrumbs (about 14 pulses)

METHOD

- Adjust oven racks to upper and lower-middle positions. Line 2 half-sheet pans with parchment paper.

- Whisk flour, baking soda, baking powder, and salt together in a medium bowl; set aside.

- Beat butter until creamy. Add both sugars; beat until fluffy, about 3 minutes, stopping to scrape down the bowl as necessary.

- Beat in peanut butter until fully incorporated; then beat in eggs, one at a time; then vanilla and molasses.

- Gently stir dry ingredients into the peanut butter mixture. Add ground peanuts and stir gently until just incorporated.

- Working with a generous 1 tablespoon at a time, roll the dough with your hands into 1-inch balls. Place balls on prepared sheets, spacing them 2 inches apart. Press each dough ball twice with a dinner fork dipped in cold water, making a crisscross design.

- Bake until cookies are puffed and slightly browned around the edges but not the top, about 12 minutes. Cool on baking sheet until set, about 4 minutes, then transfer to a wire rack.

"My husband and I loved the peanutty flavor and chewy texture. These are now our favorite peanut butter cookies, too!"
ANNA GANAHL, *an intermediate cook eager to master basics and try new recipes*

QUICK OATMEAL COOKIES

These cookies were my stepmom Margie's favorites. They are crisper than the original recipe in *The Joy of Cooking*, due to a change in the sugar proportions. Best to double this recipe, as the cookies are amazingly good. You can leave the batter covered in the refrigerator up to 1 week and bake as needed. These also freeze well in a long roll that can be cut into thin slices and baked.

Makes 2 to 3 dozen cookies, depending on size

Preheat oven to 350°.

INGREDIENTS
½ cup (1 stick) unsalted butter, slightly softened
¼ cup brown sugar
¾ cup granulated sugar
1 egg
1 teaspoon vanilla extract
1 tablespoon milk
1 cup flour
½ teaspoon baking soda
½ teaspoon baking powder
½ teaspoon salt
1 cup uncooked oats (do not use instant)
¾ cup chocolate chips
1 teaspoon orange zest (best to use a microplane for this)

METHOD
– In a stand mixer, cream butter with both sugars until smooth. Add the egg, vanilla, and milk.

– In small bowl, sift together flour, baking soda, baking powder, and salt. Add to wet ingredients and blend.

– Add the oats, chocolate chips, and orange zest, and beat well.

– Drop cookies (I make them small, about 1 teaspoon) onto parchment-lined half-sheet pans, 2 inches apart. Bake 10 to 12 minutes, until light brown.

MASAKO'S NUT COOKIES

Masako Yatabe Thomsen has baked with Sumi Chang for more than ten years, contributing a number of exceptional baked goods to Europane's repertoire. These cookies are healthy enough to be eaten with a sense of virtue and so delicious that it is difficult to stop. Therein lies the conundrum.

Makes 2 to 3 dozen cookies, depending on size

Preheat oven to 350°.

INGREDIENTS
A total of 14 ounces of the following; nuts can be lightly roasted or unroasted
   Sliced almonds
   Walnuts, chopped
   Hazelnuts, chopped
   Pistachios, chopped
   Cashews, chopped
   Pecans, chopped
   Pumpkin seeds
   Sunflower seeds
¼ cup all-purpose flour
¼ teaspoon cinnamon
½ teaspoon orange zest (a coarse microplane works well)
½ cup granulated sugar
2 large egg whites
3 tablespoons plus 1 teaspoon unsalted butter, melted

METHOD
– In a medium bowl, mix nuts, flour, cinnamon, and orange zest.

– Mix sugar and egg whites in a stainless metal bowl that will fit over a saucepan partially filled with hot water, or in a double boiler over low heat, until sugar is completely dissolved. I use a whisk and stir energetically to avoid "scrambled eggs."

– Add sugar and egg mixture to nut mixture. Mix gently with a rubber spatula.

– Stir in melted butter.

– Drop dough in 2-inch or larger dollops onto parchment-lined half-sheet pan.

– Flatten with a fork. It helps to dip the fork in cold water to avoid sticking.

– Bake 15 to 17 minutes, until cookies are golden brown.

NOTE: It is not necessary to use all the nuts and seeds listed. Consider color, texture, and taste combinations. Masako typically uses about four types. I weigh the nuts separately from the seeds, which stay whole. Then I chop the nuts together with a large knife. I like the nuts chopped relatively small, but not so fine as to lose the delightful texture. If nuts are too coarsely chopped, the cookie batter does not hold together well.

FOOD SOURCES: Aladdin Nuthouse for the highest-quality, freshest nuts; Sprouts Farmers Market, farmers' markets.

ALMOND STICKS WITH COCOA NIBS: "The Better Biscotti"

Based on a recipe in *Bittersweet: Recipes and Tales from a Life in Chocolate,* by Alice Medrich.

Makes about 25 to 30 6- to 8-inch sticks

INGREDIENTS

¾ cup blanched almonds, lightly toasted
½ cup all-purpose flour
½ cup whole-wheat pastry flour
¼ cup demerara sugar
⅓ cup granulated sugar
6 tablespoons unsalted butter, cut into ½-inch pieces
1 teaspoon vanilla extract
⅛ teaspoon almond extract
¼ cup cocoa nibs

METHOD

– Combine almonds, flours, and sugars in a food processor; pulse until almonds are the texture of fine meal.

– Add butter and pulse until mixture forms small crumbs.

– Combine 2 tablespoons water with vanilla and almond extracts, then add to processor, pulsing until dough looks damp. Add cocoa nibs and pulse until dispersed.

– Pour out the crumbly dough onto a piece of foil or parchment paper, pressing dough together into an 8 x 8-inch square about ½ inch thick.

– Wrap in a large piece of foil and let rest in the refrigerator for 2 hours or as long as overnight.

– When ready to bake, preheat oven to 350°.

– With a very sharp knife, trim dough on all sides to even it up. Then cut ⅜-inch slices, carefully transferring slices to a parchment-lined half-sheet pan with the edge of the knife.

– Bake, rotating sheets from top to bottom and front to back, 12 to 20 minutes (depending on your oven). Cookies should be golden brown at the edges and a bit darker on the bottom.

– Carefully transfer cookies to cooling racks. When cool, store in an airtight container. They taste good for at least 1 week, but won't last that long.

NOTE: Cocoa nibs are not chocolate chips. They are chocolate in its purest form, before anything else is added, and as such, are not sweet. They are dried and fermented bits of cacao beans with the texture of roasted coffee beans.

FOOD SOURCES: Cocoa nibs can be purchased at Jane's Cake and Chocolate Supply, Sprouts Farmers Market, and Surfas Culinary District.

Almond Sticks with shortbread cookies made from dough left over from Sumi Chang's Lemon Bars (see page 212).

ALMOND ANGEL COOKIES

An easy and quick cookie recipe.

Makes 4 to 5 dozen cookies

Preheat oven to 375°.

INGREDIENTS

1¾ cups whole shelled almonds, finely ground (a food processor works well); do not
   use blanched almonds
1½ cups sugar
3 large egg whites
1 teaspoon almond extract
1 teaspoon vanilla extract
Sliced almonds (optional)

METHOD

– In the bowl of a food processor using the cutting blade, combine ground almonds,
  sugar, and egg whites. Mix in extracts.

– Roll small pieces of dough—½ teaspoon each—in your hands to make very
  small balls. If dough is too gloppy, use a small spoon. Place on parchment-lined half-
  sheet pan.

– If you want to be obsessive, flatten each ball with dampened fingers and gently press
  a few sliced almonds on top.

– Bake until just brown on top, about 15 minutes.

– Remove from oven and place pans on wire racks for 5 to 10 minutes. With a spatula,
  remove cookies from pan while slightly warm; place on wire rack to cool.

– Baked cookies keep very well for at least 2 weeks. You can also keep batter in the
  refrigerator for up to 1 week and bake as needed.

NOTE: Use parchment, or you will be scraping this sweet thing off a cookie sheet
for hours.

FOOD SOURCES: Aladdin Nuthouse for the highest-quality, freshest nuts; Sprouts
Farmers Market, farmers' markets.

Polvorones (see page 214) and Chocolate Chile Truffles go well together.

CHOCOLATE CHILE TRUFFLES

Adapted from a recipe that used lavender instead of chile, and pistachios instead of cocoa powder.

Makes about 2 dozen truffles

INGREDIENTS

14 ounces good-quality semisweet chocolate chips
1 cup heavy cream or heavy whipping cream
4 small dried red chiles, seeds removed (Tien Tsin or arbol chiles work well)
½ teaspoon vanilla extract
½ cup sugar
About 1/2 cup unsweetened cocoa powder

METHOD

– Place chocolate in a medium heat-proof bowl.

– In a heavy saucepan over low heat, bring cream, chiles, vanilla, and sugar to a low boil.

– Remove from heat and pour cream mixture through a sieve into the chocolate; stir until fully incorporated. Chocolate should be fully melted and will become glossy.

– Lightly coat an 8 x 8-inch glass or metal pan with olive oil; pour chocolate mixture evenly into pan. (The pan should be small enough to fit on your freezer shelf.)

– Freeze, uncovered, 35 to 40 minutes. The cooler the truffle mixture, the easier it is to form into truffle balls. If too warm, it becomes a gooey mess. It helps to return mixture to the freezer to harden up during this process. Cut chilled mixture into 1-inch cubes, then roll cubes into balls. If you want a smaller truffle, just cut a smaller cube.

– Roll balls in the cocoa powder. Store in a tightly closed plastic container in the refrigerator up to 2 weeks.

NOTE: The heat level of dried red chiles is quite varied, so do experiment a bit. I have tested my chiles by tasting the infused hot milk. Add 2 or 3 chiles and then taste; add more depending on your taste buds. Remember, truffles are called truffles because they look rustic and uneven, like their namesakes. They should not be perfect spheres.

"Chocolate flavor at first taste, then chile kick. Yummy!"
ANNA GANAHL, *an intermediate cook eager to master basics and try new recipes*

STICKY CANDY

This recipe came from a Ralston Purina cereal box. It was passed down to my stepmom, Margie, by her grandma and is more than 100 years old. We make it during the Christmas holiday season without fail.

Makes 40 to 50 pieces of candy

Preheat oven to 350°.

INGREDIENTS

2 cups blanched, slivered almonds
3 cups brown sugar
½ cup molasses
⅓ cup whole milk
⅓ pound unsweetened baking chocolate, coarsely chopped
½ cup (1 stick) salted butter, plus more for greasing pan

METHOD

– Pour almonds onto half-sheet pan and heat in oven until roasted, about 5 to 8 minutes. Cool almonds and spread them on a buttered half-sheet pan.

– In a heavy-bottomed saucepan (cast-iron works well) over medium heat, bring sugar, molasses, and milk to a boil. Stir to combine. Immediately stir in chocolate and then butter. Stop stirring.

– Continue to cook, *without stirring*, until mixture reaches the firm- to hard-ball stage. I test the candy's doneness in two ways. Drop ½ teaspoon or so of the hot candy into very cold water. It should make strings and easily form a ball with a slightly crisp exterior. Or use a candy thermometer. The candy is done when the temperature reaches 250°.

– Pour mixture over almonds. (As the pan is heavy, make sure to grab someone with strong arms.)

– When cool, about 20 to 30 minutes, pull candy off pan and break or cut into 1-inch pieces, depending on the hardness of the candy. Pieces will be uneven, which is part of this candy's charm.

– Wrap candy pieces in cellophane, or leave on a platter for foraging family members. Wrapping is the hardest part of making Sticky Candy. Get a friend to help and watch a good movie while wrapping.

NOTE: Candy making is not hard, but understanding the various stages of the candy's temperature in relationship to the finished product helps. I test the candy's doneness frequently to avoid under- or overcooking.

Firm ball (soft caramel candy) 244° to 248°
Hard ball (nougat) 250° to 266°
Soft crack (salt water taffy) 270° to 289°
Hard crack (toffee) 295° to 309°

THE SEARCH FOR GREAT INGREDIENTS

> "I love going out of my way, beyond what I know, and finding my way back a few extra miles, by another trail, with a compass that argues with the map . . . ."
> REBECCA SOLNIT, *A Field Guide to Getting Lost*

This list is by no means a comprehensive account of the quality merchants on L.A.'s eastside. Rather, it reflects my intentional wanderings, along with recommendations from our eastside food makers: Jack Aghoian, Sumi Chang, Rumi Mahmood, Minh Phan, and Mario Rodriguez. I'm including these resources as examples that will hopefully inspire and serve as a guide to explore your own communities. Beginning with your immediate neighborhood and moving outward, look around for a small store that looks interesting, then stop and dare yourself to try something new. Ask friends who cook where they shop, especially if they are experienced in a particular culinary tradition. And if you have the time and inclination, look for an area that is particularly rich in food resources and make a day of it. These activities can become a source of joy and connection—and a great way to support your community.

Lest you feel that I do nothing but drive from store to store, I advocate for a well-stocked pantry as a basis for your cooking endeavors. Recipes often require only one or two specialty ingredients. For these, you can pick up that one item on your way home from work or pleasure when time is short. Carry a well-insulated shopping bag: a reminder and enabler of your willingness to be inspired.

One exception to the eastside cooking resources is field trips. The two listed here are side trips on your way to points north. If you are in Ojai on a Sunday morning, do find your way to its farmers' market, located downtown just north of Main Street. This is a gorgeous market, filled with local farmers' bounty. Another worthy alternative to the anonymous 101 is to drive north on Highway 126, which winds through a fertile valley of farms and small towns. In strawberry season—late May through June—look for sellers of Oxnard-grown strawberries. These are small, solid, and dark red inside—a different eating experience altogether.

1. 168 Market
There are so many Asian markets now located in the San Gabriel Valley that it is difficult to select one over another. This market is recommended often by Asian specialty cooks and others well versed in kitchen technique. I find it a clean, well-organized, and fully equipped market, with aisles of noodles and rice, unusual produce, a wide variety of seafood, and just about any condiment you might need.
1421 E. Valley Blvd., Alhambra 91801, (626) 282-5168.

2. Aladdin Nuthouse
This is one of Washington Boulevard's immaculate shops, with a delicious variety of freshly roasted nuts, dried fruit, nougat, and coffee. Prices are competitive; the quality is consistently high; and Gary Karalekian, the shop-owner, provides great service. I never leave without the delicious Persian pistachios or a piece of nougat. Gary also puts together great holiday baskets.
1647 E. Washington Blvd., Pasadena 91104, (626) 794-7533.

3. Altadena Farmers Market
A tiny, very carefully curated market with ten or so produce stands and meat purveyors. Come for a snack or light dinner, as there are several high-quality prepared-food stands. The smallness of the market means inconsistent booth coverage by the purveyors, so flexibility is the order of the day.
600 W. Palm St., Altadena 91001.
Wednesday: Fall and winter, 3 to 7 p.m.; spring and summer, 4 to 8 p.m.

4. Armen Market
How about an immaculate market with excellent produce, an in-house butcher, well-stocked delicatessen, excellent packaged goods (flour, sugar, cookies, Armenian delights), where you can pretty much get in and out of the place in about fifteen minutes? Or you can turn this into a food field trip and stay as long as you like. Did I mention it's also reasonably priced?
1873 N. Allen Ave., Pasadena 91104, (626) 794-2999.

5. Atwater Village Farmers' Market
Atwater's market is just the right size for me. Big enough for a variety of very high-quality farm, meat, and dairy purveyors, but small enough to make it an easy experience. I like to park a good distance from the market to avoid the crowd, shop at the market, and then have breakfast at one of the many excellent cafés along Glendale Boulevard.
3528 Larga Ave., Atwater 90039.

6. Berolina Bakery & Pastry Shop
Walk through the door and you enter a small town in Europe. The bread selection is extensive, ranging from Swedish limpa to rye and olive; traditional pastries include Danish and the marzipan-covered princess cake. Berolina serves breakfast and lunch to a relaxed crowd. It is next door to Schreiner's Fine Sausages and just down the street from Novin Herbs & Spices,

which makes shopping here more than worth the trip.
3421 Ocean View Blvd., Glendale 91208, (818) 249-6506.

7. Bhanu Indian Grocery and Cuisine

Bhanu offers a large variety of fresh and packaged Indian food ingredients, as well as a tasty sampling of ready-to-eat food. They serve dosas and sell the batter, which is exciting to me—as this delicate Indian crêpe is high on the list of my many food obsessions.

7246 Rosemead Blvd., San Gabriel 91775, (626) 291-2101.

8. The Cheese Cave

I like food lore, and this is a good story. Owners Marnie and Lydia Clarke are the granddaughters of the original Alta Dena Dairy owner, Harold Stueve. He was an early champion of raw milk, a controversy that forced him out of business. Both Cheese Cave locations have a large selection of cheeses, many of them from California. The team's knowledge means many teachable moments for customers.

325 Yale Ave., Claremont 91711, (909) 625-7560.
317 S. Broadway #45, Downtown Los Angeles 90013,
(213) 290-3060.

9. Los Cinco Puntos

This grocery store and deli, known and loved for its delicious house-made tacos and tamales, is named after the five-way intersection—Los Cinco Puntos—that commemorates important historic events on the eastside: The site honors Mexican American veterans of World War II, the Korean War, and the Vietnam War, and, as a counterpoint, recognizes the seminal Chicano Moratorium march in protest of the Vietnam War. You can purchase essentials—tortillas, masa, and chiles—here and eat lunch, too.

3300 E. Cesar E. Chavez Ave., Boyle Heights 90063,
(323) 261-4084.

10. Claro's Italian Markets

Great quality and variety. Bread, cheese, wonderful sausages, olives, oil, vinegar, and fun cooking equipment. Also ready-made pasta that is quite good, along with marinara and other traditional sauces. Multiple locations throughout L.A.'s eastside.

11. Cookbook

Two small markets with fresh produce, fresh eggs, cheese, charcuterie, bread, and some pantry basics, including olive oil, pasta, butter, and yogurt. These are not bargain stores; however, the quality is the highest and most consistent I have found anywhere. Owners Marta Teegen and husband Robert Stelzner have visited each of the small, sustainable farms—all within four hours from the stores—from which they source their food. Handcrafted cooking tools reinforce Cookbook's focus on quality.

5611 N. Figueroa St., Highland Park 90042, (323) 507-2051.
1549 Echo Park Ave., Echo Park 90026, (213) 250-1900.

12. Culture Club 101

This store and educational center is a beautiful space with a large dine-in area of health-oriented foods, much of it probiotic and fermented. A curated selection of organic dairy and meat products is also available. I buy raw kefir and excellent eggs here. The owner is friendly and readily answers any questions.

1392 E. Washington Blvd., Pasadena 91104, (626) 893-5164.

13. Eagle Rock Italian Bakery and Deli

Delicious cannoli and cookies, all reasonably priced, along with a small grocery store of Italian food essentials and a busy deli counter for takeout sandwiches and salads. A local business that has lasted because the quality is good, prices are low, and service is consistently attentive.

1726 Colorado Blvd., Eagle Rock 90041, (323) 255-8224.

14. Europane Bakery

Although sold recently, Europane continues to turn out great bread and pastries and offers a dine-in breakfast and lunch menu, including the signature open-face egg salad sandwich created by its founder, Sumi Chang.

345 E. Colorado Blvd., Pasadena 91101, (626) 844-8804.
950 E. Colorado Blvd., Pasadena 91106, (626) 577-1828.

15. Fish King

Very high-quality fresh fish, including seafood of all types, as well as chicken. Whenever I ask chefs where they buy fish, this market is consistently recommended. I often buy several pounds of chicken necks and backs to make homemade chicken stock. Fish King recently opened a full-service eat-in counter for an excellent and reasonably priced lunch on the run.

722 N. Glendale Ave., Glendale 91206, (818) 244-2161.

16. El Gallo Bakery

In business since 1949, El Gallo Bakery is located across the street from two sister restaurants, Moles La Tia and El Gallo Grill. Having tasted the mole at Moles La Tia, I was not surprised by the excellent quality at El Gallo. You enter the bakery, inspect the shelves carefully, and line up to order. I am often helped by friendly folk waiting as well—that's how I tried a homely little bun infused with freshly ground cinnamon that was absolutely addictive. The tamales, made by hand at Moles La Tia, are delicious—soft masa with pork, chicken, and cheese fillings.

4546 E. Cesar E. Chavez Ave., East Los Angeles 90022,
(323) 263-5528.

17. Garni Meat Market

They rise early at Garni to make rubs, marinades, and several delicious condiments, including roast pepper sauce. Perfectly butchered meat includes typical items—pork chops, lamb, beef—and the more unusual, such as quail. Alex Khachoyan, the owner, will cook meat to order.

1715 E. Washington Blvd., Pasadena 91104, (626) 798-2676.

18. Grand Central Market

L.A.'s first food hall, aptly titled Grand Central Market, debuted in 1917 and has kept pace with downtown L.A.'s fortunes and demographics over the years. Its makeover in 2011, initiated by owner Adele Yellen and "curators" Joseph Shuldiner and Kevin West, reenergized a struggling market. The tenants, including cafés and grocers of all types, have engaged a large following, including the elusive downtown-dweller market. Those selling food ingredients range from legacy folk to new; what they have in common is high quality. Try Belcampo Meat Co.; Chiles Secos; Clark Street Bread; District Market; DTLA Cheese and Kitchen; La Huerta for candy, dried fruit, and nuts; Torres Produce; and Valerias for fresh moles, spices, dried fruit, and nuts. Reasonably priced on-site parking.
317 S. Broadway, Downtown Los Angeles 90013, (213) 624-2378.

19. Grist and Toll

A small storefront with milling operations on-site. Proprietor Nan Kohler sells carefully sourced and milled local heirloom wheat and grain. This is the place to try out and then get hooked on wheat, corn, barley, and teff that truly make a difference in the quality and taste of your baking and cooking.
990 S. Arroyo Pkwy., Pasadena 91105, (626) 441-7400.

20. H Mart

This market elevates the trend of dining-in while shopping to new heights, with at least three locations to sample Korean cuisine, dumplings, and patisserie. The store itself is a wonderland of produce, mostly whole fish and shellfish—quite a bit of it wild—an aisle of rice, meats prepared for barbecue, and, of course, pickled vegetables. H Mart is both inspiring and informative. Go here to learn about the vast world of Asian cuisines.
1101 W. Huntington Dr., Arcadia 91107, (626) 241-9300.

21. Hollywood Farmers' Market

Described by many, including my foodie friends, as the best farmers' market in Los Angeles, this is certainly the most extensive, with more than 160 farmers, producers, and food stalls. I often see chefs rushing by with large boxes of greens; many stop to chat with one another. Be prepared to walk slowly, carry a big bag, and take a friend. This experience moves us well beyond an errand; it is a form of communion with excellence. Minh Phan's list of participants at the market is indicative: Bernard Family Farm, Farmer Mai, Flora Bella Farm, Givens Farm (also at the Atwater Village Farmers' Market), Koda Farms, Thao Family Farm, McGrath Family Farm, Shear Rock Farms, T & D Farms, Underwood Family Farms, Weiser Family Farms, and Yasutomi Farms.
1600 Ivar Ave., Hollywood 90028. Sunday, 8 a.m. to 1 p.m.

22. India Food and Spices

This is an immaculate store, with excellent produce, whole and ground spices, pickles, nuts, and unusual types of rice sold in bulk. The store manager is helpful and will describe how many of the lesser-known vegetables can enhance flavor. To make the trip eastward all the more worthwhile, the eat-in area features dosa—India's crêpes that are so very good. Yes, I am obsessed.
2221 Huntington Dr., Duarte 91010, (626) 357-6899.

23. Jane's Cake and Chocolate Supply

For all you bakers with the skill and fortitude to try fondant, layer cakes, and character cakes—or, for those of you like me, who are content simply to admire the large selection of flavor extracts and baking chocolate—Jane's is the place for you.
645 Foothill Blvd., La Canada 91011, (818) 790-5900 (located along the walkway behind Gelson's Supermarket).

24. Victor Jaramillo's Honey Stand

Victor describes himself as the "oldest beekeeper in the world," which may be true, as he is in his nineties. As a young boy in Zacatecas, Mexico, he experienced his first honey harvest riding on his father's back; he soon discovered a talent for finding bee swarms. Here, his bees rest at night in a jumble of hives scattered around the front and side of his old wood-frame house; they "work" during the day in nearby locales—the hills of El Sereno and Bouquet Canyon and gardens in South Pasadena. Victor sells his honey every Saturday and some Mondays during daylight hours. It is, as he says, "the best honey in the world."
Next door to El Sereno Library, at 5226 S. Huntington Dr., El Sereno 90032.

25. Julienne

Lovely, relaxing, and primarily a café with consistently delicious food, Julienne is on this list because of its baked goods—that bread!—and owner Julie Campoy's brilliant understanding of what it means to create and nourish community.
2649 Mission St., San Marino 91108, (626) 441-2290.

26. The King's Roost

Owner Roe Sie is a passionate urban homesteader and bread baker. His small store includes wheat berries and other whole organic heirloom grains. A countertop grain mill is among the tools he sells to encourage self-sufficiency. The King's Roost offers classes in bread-baking and other satisfying forms of DIY; the store also hosts the bulk-ordering program for Los Angeles Bread Bakers, a group of amateur and professional bakers, at extremely reasonable prices. Buy a bag and share it with friends.
3732 Sunset Blvd., Silver Lake 90026, (323) 426-9769.

27. Lincoln

Christine Moore's "second child"—sister to Little Flower—an airy, happy space filled with community folk chowing down on everything from warm bulgur with cream to salads, amazing fried-egg sandwiches on brioche, and layer cake. And then there are the breads and pastries. Yum! Avoid Saturday and Sunday mornings if you can, unless you enjoy crowds.
1992 Lincoln Ave., Pasadena 91103, (626) 765-6746.

Carolyn Echter, store manager of Cookbook's Highland Park location.

Bins of freshly roasted nuts at Aladdin Nuthouse.

La Mayordomia Market owner Zeferino Garcia.

28. Little Flower

Christine Moore's first venture is an intimate spot, always comforting and delicious, with baked savory and sweet delights similar to Lincoln. In both Lincoln and Little Flower, attention to detail and an evolving menu attract new customers and keep the regulars coming back.

1422 W. Colorado Blvd., Pasadena 91105, (626) 304-4800.

29. Marukai Market

Located in Weller Court in Little Tokyo, the market looks more like a toy and novelty store upon entering. Just keep moving toward the perimeter and the rear, and you will find some surprises, including Negi onions, a Japanese version of the green onion that appears in the spring and is a key ingredient for Minh Phan's Negi Oil (see page 48). The rice and vinegar selection is vast, with products from Koda and Echigoya rice farms of special note. Although the store is relatively small, its merchandise is often choice. Parking costs are high, so make a day of it—there is lots to see.

123 S. Onizuka St. #105, Little Tokyo 90012, (213) 893-7200.

30. La Mayordomia Market

There are two Mayordomia markets, but this one near Truffle Brothers and Surfas completes a trifecta that represents some of the best food shopping on L.A.'s eastside. At this market, you will find great produce, a butcher, an excellent bakery, and fresh masa for tortillas and tamales. Owner Zeferino Garcia aptly calls his stores la mayordomia, meaning "stewardship" in English. This is one of the most aesthetic markets I have ever experienced, and everything is very, very fresh, delicious, and reasonably priced. Hang out and watch what the regulars buy; then ask and try.

3301 W. Pico Blvd., Arlington Heights 91109, (323) 766-0575.

31. El Mercado de Los Angeles

I am an inveterate market fan—someone who actually feels my heart beat faster as I walk through the door. El Mercado, established in 1968, is just such a place: a visual feast of vendors selling masa, ready-made moles, extensive produce, meat, and kitchen housewares. The latter includes comals and tortilla presses of all types. Invest in a lengthy visit; you will learn as well as enjoy. Eat-in areas throughout provide another way to learn about Mexican, Central, and South American cuisine. Bring cash, as most vendors do not take plastic.

3425 E. 1st St., Boyle Heights 90063. (323) 268-3451.

32. Milkfarm

An excellent artisanal cheese shop, founded by Leah Park Fierro. She is committed to sourcing quality ingredients—locally, whenever possible. Cheese and charcuterie are cut to order. Look for special events and classes, and do try her version of a grilled cheese sandwich while shopping—it's not your mother's Velveeta.

2106 Colorado Blvd., Eagle Rock 90041, (323) 892-1068.

33. Namaste Spiceland

A well-stocked store primarily for Indian cuisine, along with various curries and dahls to eat in or take away. Don't let the unruly stacks of rice bags in the front window put you off; all is orderly and clean inside.

270 N. Hill Ave., Pasadena 91106, (626) 345-5514.

34. Nicole's Market & Café

Consistently authentic, well-made bistro fare, along with a good selection of cheeses, mostly French and Spanish. Nicole Grandjean is from the Loire Valley and so knows her cheeses; look for a small but well-curated selection always displayed at optimum ripeness. A refined sampling of French grocery items is also available, including oil, vinegar, wine, and baking ingredients—all essentials in my book. Nicole is generous with her knowledge about selections and serving.

921 Meridian Ave., South Pasadena 91030, (626) 403-5751.

35. Now Serving

If you are in the market for any culinary title, look no further. Within its 450-square-foot space, Now Serving offers the rare and wonderful: cookbooks—newly published and historic—as well as a thoughtful selection of knives, chef's tweezers, serving dishes, aprons, and more. Owners Ken Concepcion and Michelle Mungcal see their shop as an essential for Los Angeles—one of the world's greatest food cities.

Far East Plaza, 727 N. Broadway #133, Chinatown 90012, (213) 395-0627.

If walking, it is easier to enter the Plaza from Hill Street.

36. Panaderia Delicia

Thanks to the growing number of panaderias serving pan dulce (sweet bread) on the eastside, the drill is pretty familiar. You walk in, see what strikes your fancy—elotito (cornbread), conchas, or crusty-on-the-outside, soft-on-the-inside bolillos—take a tray and tongs, and have at it. Delicia stands out for the quality and freshness of its baked goods. It is one of Mario Rodriguez's recommendations, and he is never wrong about these things. Prices are very reasonable.

5567 N. Figueroa St., Highland Park 90042, (323) 259-9306.

37. Papa Cristo's

If you happen to be in the Arlington Heights area, home to many of the resources on this list, do visit this Greek emporium and eating hall with its easy parking. The deli is the real star here, with its bakery items, cheese, and charcuterie. And then there is the dizzying selection of olive oil. The response from the counter guy to all of my questions was, "Try it." So I did, and walked out with several new favorites.

2771 W. Pico Blvd., Arlington Heights 90006, (323) 737-2970.

38. Pasadena Certified Farmers' Market at Victory Park

This market sprawls within the parking lot of Pasadena High School. It has a large number of excellent produce stands, many of them organic, along with egg farmers, fish mongers, organic butchers, and cheese and poultry folk. While large enough to include variety, it is an easy market to navigate, and parking is rational.

Sierra Madre Blvd. at Paloma St., Pasadena 91107. Saturday, 8:30 a.m. to 12:30 p.m.

39. La Princesita Carnicera y Tortilleria

A small shop that specializes in meat prepared for Mexican cuisine, including marinated beef for carne asada, pork trimmed for pozole, Milanese cutlets, goat, and ground meats. The tortillas are considered the best of the machine-made by those in the know (including Wes Avila of Guerrilla Tacos!), as they cook, steam, and grind their own corn.

3432 E. Cesar E. Chavez Ave., East Los Angeles 90063, (323) 267-0673.

40. Proof Bakery

The precision and aesthetic sensibility of her early studies in art history are reflected in Na Young Ma's masterful pastry baking. Everything I eat at Proof is a revelation. She understands laminated dough and traditional techniques, but the flavors themselves are seasonal, inspired by the plentiful, year-round produce of Southern California. Try a croissant and anything that includes seasonal fruit.

3156 Glendale Blvd., Atwater 90039, (323) 664-8633.

41. Punjab Indian Grocery Store

A small, well-stocked grocery store with a focus on lentils, beans, and other vegetarian foods. The people behind the counter are helpful and enjoy advising us newbies about Indian flavors—a very comfortable place to get to know a cuisine that might be new to you.

1300 E. Main St., Alhambra 91801, (626) 576-0749.

42. Rincon Argentino

Yum all around! Great meat, including various sausages, delicious savory and sweet pastries, and unusual and intriguing products from Argentina. This is another small family-owned jewel that makes shopping for ingredients truly enjoyable.

1375 E. Colorado St., Glendale 91205, (818) 246-4562.

43. Roma Italian Deli and Grocery

Rosario Mazzeo deserves to be recognized here, having owned this deli and market for sixty years. The place is packed at lunchtime for "The Sandwich." I go for the fairly priced, excellent cheese and Italian deli meat, including prosciutto and pancetta, as well as hard-to-find items such as *bottarga*, salt-cured fish roe. Many pantry goods are available as well, including polenta, olive oil, olives, and anchovies. In the summer—if you are lucky—you will find some of the amazingly delicious peaches that Rosario imports: "The best in the world."

918 N. Lake Ave., Pasadena 91104, (626) 797-7748.

44. Say Cheese

I love Say Cheese for so many reasons: owner Glenn Harrell's kindness and interest in teaching; the vast variety of charcuterie delights and great year-round and seasonal cheese; and delicious, very generous sandwiches made on the premises. He will also provide cheese options at various price points without disdain.

2800 Hyperion Ave., Silver Lake 90027, (323) 665-0545.

45. Schreiner's Fine Sausages

This great store sells its own house-made sausages and an enormous variety of deli meats. It is strong on pork and beef, all of which is beautifully butchered and very, very fresh. Service is efficient and friendly. My husband purchases casings and fat for his homemade sausages, another reason to be grateful to Schreiner's.

3417 Ocean View Blvd., Glendale 91208, (818) 244-4735.

46. Seed Bakery

A delightful addition to the Washington Boulevard "foodie corridor." Joseph Abrakjian, the owner, bakes with artisanal whole grains that are milled on-site, and uses a natural levain rising technique. These efforts make you feel good about your bread eating, but the resulting deliciousness is what brings the growing number of customers back. Pastries, especially croissants, and a small café menu are imaginative and very tasty.

942 E. Washington Blvd., Pasadena 91104, (626) 486-2115.

47. Semolina Artisanal Pasta

Leah Ferrazzani recently relocated her small storefront artisanal pasta-making operation to northwest Pasadena, next door to Lincoln. Semolina uses only organic durum wheat; special bronze dies to extrude the pasta for a rough, sauce-loving texture; and slow-drying techniques. Here's where the rubber hits the road for me: This is delicious pasta that competes handily with homemade, and while it costs more than store-bought, its quality is well worth the price. A growing shelf of complementary food items, including sauces, rounds out the experience.

1976 Lincoln Ave., Pasadena 91103, (323) 352-8564. Semolina also has a booth at the Hollywood Farmers' Market.

48. Spain Restaurant Los Angeles

I cannot count how many times I have passed this small restaurant and market on my way south from the Glendale Freeway. This is a very good place to try authentic Spanish food and to purchase key ingredients such as bomba rice, chorizo, and cheese.

1866 Glendale Blvd., Echo Park 90026, (323) 667-9045.

Roma Deli owner Rosario Mazzeo, slicing meat for "The Sandwich."

A tray of deliciousness at Proof Bakery in Atwater.

Glenn Harrell at Say Cheese in Silver Lake.

Seed Bakery owners Joseph Abrakjian, baker, and his wife, Pam Watanabe.

A sample of baseball-size "winter" truffles at Truffle Brothers.

Truffle Brothers Marco and Michael Pietroiacovo.

49. Sprouts Farmers Market

For convenience and an excellent dairy section, Sprouts is it. This store has connections with some of California's best dairy farmers, and it's where I buy raw milk, excellent yogurt, and better-quality goat's milk to make cheese. The produce is very fairly priced and often organic.
Locations throughout L.A.'s eastside and beyond.

50. Super A Foods

What a great market! It is well-organized, with ready-to-eat food, delicious Mexican cheeses and crema, a long butcher counter, and a vast produce section. There are the more typical offerings—papayas, oranges, limes, cilantro, lettuce, onions—along with the unusual, including prickly pear and taro root. The meat department includes various cuts of beef, pork, and chicken prepared for asada and milanesa.
5250 York Blvd., Highland Park 90042, (323) 551-6884 and locations throughout L.A.'s eastside.

51. Super King Market

Nicknamed the United Nations of Supermarkets, Super King is representative of the glorious polyglot food scene that continues to evolve on L.A.'s eastside. I go for the excellent produce and the food cultures that make our community so exciting. Two caveats: The meats are not well butchered, so I avoid that counter. You may also want to avoid weekends, when congested parking may color your experience of the grand interior.
2260 Lincoln Ave., Altadena 91001, (626) 296-9311.

52. Surfas Culinary District

It's back! Surfas recently relocated to L.A.'s Arlington Heights neighborhood, making this one of the greatest concentrations of food purveyors in the city—who knew? The store is laid out differently from its previous location in Culver City, but most everything else is the same. Great deals on spices, a vast array of baker's chocolate, olive oil, grains, unusual canned and frozen goods, and excellent chef's equipment and supplies.
3225 W. Washington Blvd., Arlington Heights 90018, (310) 559-4770.

53. Truffle Brothers

Marco and Michael Pietroiacovo represent generations of truffle expertise. They come from the Molise area of Italy. Their journey from homeland to an impressive retail and wholesale operation in Los Angeles was surprisingly quick—due in part to the quality of their white and black truffles and their enthusiasm about everything truffle. Do not worry if you are not a chef; all are greeted warmly in this friendly store. There is plenty of opportunity to try the various forms of truffle-infused flavors, from cheese to salt to oils, before investing in the unadulterated version. A busy deli counter carries excellent cheese and charcuterie. Lunch in their sunny patio was absolutely delicious.
4073 W. Washington Blvd., Arlington Heights 90018, (323) 402-0478.

54. Urban Radish

As the residential population of Downtown L.A. continues to grow, the restaurant scene has taken a lead in innovative food development, but grocery stores have been slower to respond. Urban Radish is one of the newer full-service markets downtown. The store features a great cheese counter, excellent bread and produce, and nice-to-have fare, including chocolates. Easy parking adds convenience to this store's appeal, as does its proximity to the Arts District.
660 Imperial St., south of the Downtown Arts District 90021, (213) 892-1570.

55. Vallarta Supermarkets

This is a full-service market with distinctive counter service for most everything: Salsa? Sure! Tortillas and masa? Absolutely! Ceviche? How about eight varieties? The produce section is packed with the typical and the rare, and there are regular pantry basics as well, so you can have your specialized ingredients without going elsewhere for toilet paper. In other words, I shop here a lot. Prices are not the lowest but are reasonable for the quality and convenience.
665 N. Fair Oaks, Pasadena 91103, (626) 204-6960.
3425 Whittier Blvd., Boyle Heights 90023, (323) 980-4400.

FIELD TRIPS

56. America Berry

America Berry is a small company with expertise in growing strawberries, and that is it. The berries get smaller, darker, and sweeter as the season progresses. I buy mine on the way home from the Ojai Music Festival the first week of June and start sampling well before my drive is over. Look for the bright yellow sign with a big red strawberry on the south side of Highway 126 between Fillmore and Santa Paula. The stand is at the corner of Atmore Road, a few feet off the highway. A second location is adjacent to Yamaguchi's fruit and flower stand, also on the south side of Highway 126, closer to Santa Paula.
1 N. Atmore Rd., Fillmore 93015.

57. Ojai Certified Farmers' Market

I have been going to Ojai since my parents packed me and my stroller into their station wagon for the drive to the Ojai Music Festival, where we camped out in the free seats on the tennis courts. Ojai continues to feel like a special place: low-key, intimate, suffused with pink sky at dusk. The town has become decidedly more upscale, but its large farming community endures. This market has fine produce, grown just a few miles from the center of town. You will find the unusual and the familiar, all of it fresh and of exceptional quality.
300 E. Matilija St., Ojai 93023, (805) 698-5555.

Elisa Callow is first and foremost a lover of community. She is the founding executive director of the Armory Center for the Arts in Pasadena, a nationally recognized center for arts education and community development. A self-taught cook, she spent her formative years in Southeast Asia—her first foray into the world's culinary marketplaces. She completed the Pro Cooking course at the New School of Cooking and is an enthusiastic member of Los Angeles Bread Bakers. Elisa's appreciation for food and culture is evidenced through her adventurous blog, *The Urban Forager*. She is author of *The Cousins' Passover: Reflections on Fifteen Years of Celebrations* and contributing author of *Interplay: Inspiring Wonder, Discovery, and Learning through Interdisciplinary Museum-Community Partnerships*.

Ann Elliott Cutting is a professional photographer based in Pasadena. She is associate professor of photography at Art Center College of Design and leads workshops at LA Center for Photography and at the Xiem Clay Center. Ann's photography has been featured in *The Portable Feast: Creative Meals for Work and Play*, by Jeanne Kelly, *Photo District News, Graphis, Communication Arts, Los Angeles Magazine, Time Magazine, Los Angeles Times, The Washington Post*, and *Bloomberg News*.

ANN ELLIOTT CUTTING, PHOTOGRAPHER

ELISA CALLOW, AUTHOR

PHOTOGRAPH BY DENNIS KEELEY

INDEX

Gluten-Free Recipes

Vegetarian Recipes